AKC® OFFICIAL GUIDE TO
TOY DOGS

AKC® OFFICIAL GUIDE TO
TOY DOGS

Featuring Lovable Breeds including Yorkshire Terrier, Chihuahua, Papillon, and Pomeranian

AMERICAN KENNEL CLUB®

CompanionHouse BOOKS

AKC® Official Guide to Toy Dogs

CompanionHouse Books™ is an imprint of Fox Chapel Publishing.

Project Team
The American Kennel Club®, Inc.
Fox Chapel Publishing
  Editor: Madeline DeLuca
  Designer: Wendy Reynolds
  Indexer: Jay Kreider

All photos are credited to The American Kennel Club®, Inc, unless otherwise noted.

Additional Shutterstock.com images: Anna Vasiljeva (2-3); Ulia_gorbunova (5); Eudyptula (6); Volodymyr Burdiak (10-11); Evgeniia Shikhaleeva (12, 68, 82); Ksenia Raykova (14-15); DragoNika (16-17); BIGANDT.COM (19); Eric Isselee (21); Jolanta Beinarovica (22); Artsiom P (23); Yuriy Baklushyn ph (24); Emolaev Alexander (25); Alexander Sobol (27); Cavan-Images (33); Olga Aniven (34-35); KaliAntye (77); WilleeCole Photography (86); Dulova Olga (91); Daria Shvetcova (121).

American Kennel Club®, AKC®, AKC Meet the Breeds®, AKC S.T.A.R. Puppy®, AKC Rally®, AKC Scent Work®, Canine Good Citizen®, and Foundation Stock Service® are registered trademarks of The American Kennel Club.

Copyright © 2025 by the American Kennel Club®

All rights reserved. No part of this book may be reproduced, stored in a retrieval system, or transmitted in any form or by any means, electronic, mechanical, photocopying, recording, or otherwise, without the prior written permission of Fox Chapel Publishing, except for the inclusion of brief quotations in an acknowledged review.

ISBN 978-1-62187-243-6

Library of Congress Control Number: 2025932127

This book has been published with the intent to provide accurate and authoritative information in regard to the subject matter within. While every precaution has been taken in the preparation of this book, the author and publisher expressly disclaim any responsibility for any errors, omissions, or adverse effects arising from the use or application of the information contained herein. The techniques and suggestions are used at the reader's discretion and are not to be considered a substitute for veterinary care. If you suspect a medical problem, consult your veterinarian.

Fox Chapel Publishing
903 Square Street
Mount Joy, PA 17552

We are always looking for talented authors.
To submit an idea, please send a brief inquiry to acquisitions@foxchapelpublishing.com.

Printed and bound in Malaysia
First Printing

Toy dogs have been bred to sit on the laps of royalty, like this Cavalier King Charles Spaniel.

Foreword

Humans have always needed a best friend. Over the centuries—indeed millennia—various dogs have filled that need. Gradually, however, we developed dogs whose main purpose was not to hunt or herd, to guard or get dinner, but simply to provide us with companionship.

One of the largest collections of dogs that fulfill this important function is the AKC® Toy Group. These diminutive dogs may be called toys, but they are not playthings. Their small stature belies big hearts and big attitudes. Upon first glance, their size seems to be the only thing that the breeds have in common, but with a deeper look it becomes apparent that there are several subgroups of toy dogs. And, within these subgroups, there has been considerable crossing and recrossing that has led to the development of the toy breeds as we know them today.

Small companion dogs have always been part of Eastern and Western civilization. Paintings and mosaics of the rich houses of Pompeii depict a variety of small dogs as happy, cherished animals. Although the famous mosaic that reads *Cave Canem*, meaning "Beware the Dog," has been interpreted by most cynologists as a warning of guard dogs, French veterinarian and writer Fernand Mery believed otherwise. Mery championed a new school of thought which believes that *Cave Canem* was actually a warning to make sure not to step on the numerous toy dogs sleeping around the house.

The great ladies of Imperial Rome valued their lapdogs above price, and for centuries afterward, pet dogs were a privilege of the leisured classes. Indeed, the keeping of most purebred dogs was not allowed among the peasant population.

Medieval fanciers had other tasks for toy dogs besides companionship. In 1486, Dame Juliana Berners, prioress of the Sopewell Nunnery, described toy dogs as "smaller laydees poppees that bare away the fleas." In the sixteenth century, Dr. Johannes Caius, physician to Queen Elizabeth I, wrote that toy dogs should be carried to ward off sickness.

Some dogs within the Toy Group, such as the Toy Manchester Terrier and Toy Poodle, are actually toy varieties of larger cousins with the same standards. Others, such as the Pug, Shih Tzu and Pekingese, just happen to be small dogs that are not toy versions of anything else. Many of the toy breeds have, in fact, varied greatly in size over the years.

Contents

What Is the AKC®?	10
Anatomy of a Dog	16
Finding the Perfect Puppy	21
The Sport of Dogs	28
The Toy Group	34
Breed Profiles	36
Index	143

What Is the AKC®?

In September 1884, a group of sportsmen gathered in Philadelphia to establish an organization to govern dog shows in the United States. Each member of the group was a representative or "delegate" from a dog club that had, in the recent past, held a dog show or field trial. It was the birth of the American Kennel Club® (AKC®).

Since that historic meeting, the AKC®, a club of clubs, has blossomed into the world's largest registry of purebred dogs and the nation's leading not-for-profit organization devoted to the study, breeding, and advancement of all things canine.

From glamorous dog shows in spotlighted arenas to small obedience matches on summer afternoons, promoting the benefits of the purebred dog is the AKC®'s central focus, but it is far from the whole picture.

It's the love of dogs, in their infinite variety, that is the soul of the AKC®. The organization is dedicated to protecting the rights of breeders and dog owners, as well as promoting responsible dog ownership.

Among other programs, the AKC® has built the world's largest database of purebred canine DNA profiles for parentage-verification and genetic-identity purposes, like in verifying these beautiful Chihuahuas.

The Maltese is just one of many toy breeds that make a wonderful pet.

Advancing Health and Welfare

- **AKC® Canine Health Foundation (CHF):** Founded in 1995 as an independent, affiliated nonprofit organization, CHF is dedicated to advancing the health of all dogs and increasing their owners' knowledge by funding scientific research and supporting the dissemination of health information to prevent, treat, and cure canine disease.
- **AKC® Reunite:** The mission of the nation's largest nonprofit pet recovery service is to keep pet microchipping and enrollment affordable, with no annual fees, so more lost pets can find their way home. Since 1995, AKC® has helped reunite more than 600,000 lost pets with their owners. More than ten million pets (of thirty-five different species) are enrolled in the AKC® Reunite pet-recovery service. As a nonprofit, AKC® Reunite gives its profits back to the US pet community through programs including grants to support volunteer canine search and rescue organizations, microchip scanner donations to shelters and rescues, and the AKC® Pet Disaster Relief trailers that deliver nonperishable necessities for sheltering pets to local emergency-management teams. These trailers provide animal-care services during the first critical hours following a disaster, before FEMA support and services can be deployed. Additionally, AKC® Reunite's Adopt a K-9 Cop grant program matches donations from AKC® clubs to provide funds for police departments to acquire a K-9 officer.
- **AKC® Humane Fund:** The AKC® Humane Fund celebrates and supports responsible dog ownership with grants, scholarships, the Awards for Canine Excellence, and other programs. Its grants for pet-friendly domestic violence shelters and breed rescue organizations advance and uphold the human-canine bond.
- **AKC® Inspections:** The AKC® is the only purebred registry in the United States with an ongoing routine kennel-inspection program. The AKC® has a dedicated team of field agents who visit kennels to help breeders while ensuring the proper care and conditions of AKC®-registered dogs and verifying that breeders are maintaining accurate records for their dogs. Since 2000, AKC® field agents have conducted over 70,000 inspections nationwide.

Building Community

The AKC® offers a wealth of education, information, and experiences for people who love dogs, including:

- **Public Events**: AKC Meet the Breeds®, its flagship event held in New York City, introduces thousands of people to new breeds, dog sports, AKC® initiatives, and activities.
- **AKC® Education**: This department strives to be the source of knowledge for all things dog, educating the public about purebred dogs, the sport of purebred dogs, and responsible dog ownership. AKC® Education meets this goal through online courses and exams for judges, groomers, breeders, trainers, and more via the AKC® Canine College. Additionally, AKC® Public Education offers numerous programs for the community such as the AKC® Canine Ambassador Program, AKC® PupPals, and AKC® Educator Resources. Finally, informative webinars are offered free of charge monthly on topics of interest for all dog owners.
- **Award-Winning Magazines**: *AKC® Family Dog*, published six times a year, is packed with expert advice on health, grooming, behavior, and training, as well as heartwarming and inspiring tales of dogs and their owners that you will find nowhere else. *The AKC® Gazette* features breed columns for every registered AKC® breed.
- **Website**: *AKC.org*, the organization's website, gives the public 24/7 access to the world's most extensive storehouse of knowledge on all topics related to dogs. It is also the go-to place for topnotch goods and services.
- **AKC.tv**: The digital network AKC.tv features dog-related programming 24/7, as well as an on-demand library of world-class dog events, training and health tips, and original series created especially for dog owners and lovers, such as AKC Good Dog TV.
- **The AKC® Museum of the Dog**: Founded in 1980 in New York City, this AKC® gallery is the world's finest collection of dog-related art, comprising depictions of man's best friend in oil, watercolor, ink, and sculpture.

The AKC® Museum of the Dog in New York City has this life-size bronze Havanese statue on display. It is modeled after Bono, the top-winning Havanese show dog.

- **The AKC® Research Library**: Founded in 1934, this library is a unique repository of dog-related books, memorabilia, and ephemera, including many rare and antique editions, modern works, bound periodicals, and stud books from all over the world. The library presently contains more than 18,000 volumes.
- **AKC® Canine Partners**: Begun in 2009, this important program is designed to promote responsible ownership of both purebred and mixed breeds. It allows mixed breeds to enter companion events, based solely on the dogs' training and performance. There are over 500,000 dogs enrolled. Mixed breeds are eligible to title in tracking and therapy dog work, as well as flyball, Barn Hunt, dock diving, agility, and much more.

Recognizing Greatness

The AKC® honors heroes, canine and human, who have gone above and beyond the call of duty, from police dogs to community activists to fanciers who have made outstanding contributions to the improvement and preservation of their breeds. These awards include:

- **The AKC® Humane Fund Award for Canine Excellence (ACE)**: Every year since 2000, the AKC® and the AKC® Humane Fund have chosen teams who exemplify everything that's best about the canine/human bond. The categories include therapy dog, service, search and rescue, uniformed services K-9, and, of course, exemplary companion.
- **Breeder of the Year Award**: The AKC® recognizes and celebrates an outstanding purebred dog breeder with the annual Breeder of the Year Award. The award honors those breeders who have dedicated their lives to improving the health, temperament, and quality of purebred dogs. At a special presentation held during the AKC®/Royal Canin National Championship, a breeder, or pair of breeders, is recognized in each of the seven groups. At the conclusion of the presentation, one of the seven group recipients is chosen as the Breeder of the Year.
- **Lifetime Achievement Awards**: The AKC® Lifetime Achievement Awards were established in 1998 to celebrate those individuals whose many years of dedication have led to significant contributions to their breeds and the dog sport on a national level.

The AKC® has plenty of resources to help you connect with your dog, like this Russian Toy.

Anatomy of a Dog

The dog is much more than the sum of his parts. Still, it's important to remember that dogs' beauty and talents—and our emotional responses to them—have been molded over at least fifteen thousand years of evolution. Beyond the evolutionary process, selective breeding created unique looks and enhanced inborn abilities and temperament, all related to how those various parts come together. Those parts and how they are assembled have created the most versatile species on earth. Today, there are dogs for all kinds of jobs, whether it's leaping out of a helicopter to save a person who is drowning or nestling into a lap to comfort the elderly. In many ways, dogs and people are very much alike, beings composed of such stuff as bone, blood, muscle, skin, and hair. Using DNA from a Boxer named Tasha, scientists created a map of the canine genome. Comparisons to the human version have shown us that, genetically speaking, there's only about a 15-percent difference between you and your dog. That's why dogs are proving to be such excellent models for scientists seeking treatments for the worst human illnesses, such as cancer, heart disease, and arthritis.

Every part of the dogs we know today, like this Miniature Pinscher's compact body, is created for a specific purpose in that dog's life.

Breed Standards

Many spectators at dog shows wonder how judges, in the two-and-a-half minutes allocated to examine a dog in the ring, can pick a winner. What is the judge looking at when he or she peers into the dog's mouth, runs his or her hand along the dog's sides, and steps back and intently watches every step as the handler and the dog move around the ring? How does the judge choose one dog over another?

Judges evaluate dogs based on a written description of an ideal specimen, which is known as the breed standard. A dog who possesses all the best traits mentioned in the standard is said to have good *type*.

In an examination, the judge will go over each dog with his or her hands, checking for breed-type points, those physical characteristics that give the breed its unique shape, movement, and overall appearance.

It's impossible to list every anatomical point the judge will consider; there are hundreds. But following is a quick rundown of some of the highlights, as well as the terms used to describe a few variations that separate a giant, plushly coated Tibetan Mastiff from a petite, near-naked Chinese Crested.

HEAD

The shape of the skull; how the eyes are set; the size of the jaws and cheeks; color, size, and shape of the nose; size, shape, and placement of the ears, all of these are described in detail in a breed standard. These characteristics establish expression and help the dog do his job. Some experts have counted as many as forty-five different kinds of canine noggins. There are dogs whose heads have a unique structure, such as the egg-shaped appearance of the Bull Terrier or the massive skull of the Dogue de Bordeaux. Dog heads, in general, come in three basic shapes:
- brachycephalic, round and short-nosed, as seen in breeds like the Boston Terrier, Pug, and Pekingese
- dolichocephalic, long, narrow-skulled, like Borzoi, Greyhounds, and Collies
- mesaticephalic, with medium proportions, as seen in many retrievers and setters

EARS

Ears: Whether they're the oversized triangles of a Pembroke Welsh Corgi, the long, velvety flaps of the Basset Hound, or the butterfly wings that grace the head of the Papillon, ears are among the most expressive parts of the dog. The size, shape, and the ear set, (how the lobes are attached to the head) contribute a lot to the overall look. There are more than thirty terms used to describe the various canine ear shapes. Here are just a few:
- bat ear
- blunt-tipped ear
- flying ear
- folding ear

BITE

Most dogs have forty-two teeth, twenty in the upper jaw, twenty-two in the lower. When a judge looks into a dog's mouth, he or she is making sure that all the teeth are present and that the bite conforms to the breed standard. There are four basic bites, and each serves a purpose either in creating an expression or in the dog's work:
- overshot
- undershot
- level
- scissors

FRONT ASSEMBLY

The front assembly generally refers to the shoulders and the front legs. Correct form here allows the dog's legs to move out in front, what is known as reach. Ideal reach will differ between, say, a Saluki and a Bulldog, and this will be determined by the construction of the shoulders, legs, and forefeet. Judges pay special attention to angulation, the angles of bones and joints. Angulation is one of the most important aspects of canine anatomy. Correct angulation encourages proper muscular development, which makes for a dog who can move with ease.

FEET

Dogs' feet come in several shapes:
- Cat feet, compact with a short third digit, are thought to improve endurance because they are easier to lift.
- Webbed feet are good for swimming breeds like the Newfoundland, Labrador Retriever, and Portuguese Water Dog.
- Hare feet are elongated with two center toes larger than the side toes, seen in some sighthounds and toy breeds.

The Pug has a brachycephalic head.

Canine poetry in motion, a dog's gait reflects its structure, purpose, and character. Here is the Papillon.

RIB CAGE

Dogs have nine pairs of true ribs (connected directly to the breastbone), three pairs of false ribs (connected together by cartilage), and a set of floating ribs (unattached, as name implies). Judges will check for spring, the curvature in the ribs, which indicates how much space there is for heart and lungs.

REAR ASSEMBLY

The rear assembly—structure of the hindquarters—contributes to the dog's ability to thrust forward with his back legs, allowing him to sprint and leap. This is known as drive. As with the front assembly, correct angulation is extremely important. Also, the front and rear must be in balance, or the dog's movement will be impaired.

TAILS

Finally, the judge will look at the tail and the tailset (how the tail is attached to the dog's rump). As with ears, there are many different types of tails, and there's a separate ideal for each breed:
- plume
- curled
- sickle
- otter
- screw

Finding the Perfect Puppy

Adding a dog to your household is a big decision, one not to be made on impulse. The right choice may enhance your life beyond all expectations, while a bad one can mean aggravation, disappointment, and heartache. So, with the millions of puppies and dogs out there, how do you pick the right one?

Ask yourself if you're ready for a long commitment before getting a puppy, like this Shih Tzu.

Are You Ready for a Dog?

First, it's important to ask yourself some hard questions. If you have a family that includes a spouse and children, sit down with them and ask them these questions too. Nothing is sadder than a puppy purchased on impulse because "the kids wanted a dog"—a puppy who is then relegated to the backyard when the novelty wears off.

When you start to consider owning a dog, here are some of the important lifestyle questions to ask yourself:

- Do I have time for walks, training, and daily maintenance?
- Am I prepared for the expense of dog ownership, which includes regular veterinary care, such as exams and vaccinations, as well as food, bedding, training, and toys?
- Am I willing to include the dog in my life? Dogs are highly social creatures. They do best when they are actively involved in as much of their human's life as possible. A dog will not be happy sitting home all day while his people are at work, then getting a brief walk before a long night home alone again because his people like to go out after work.
- Can I make a commitment to the average ten- to twenty-year life span of most dogs?

Pick Your Breed

If you answer yes to all these questions, you next need to determine which breed of dog is best for you. That can be achieved by asking yourself how you hope to include a dog in your life:

- Are you a marathon runner looking for a jogging buddy or are you a couch potato who wants a pal to join you watching TV?
- Do you mind having to vacuum every day?
- Are you interested in getting involved in such sports as agility, field trials, or conformation dog showing?
- Would you prefer a dog who reflects your heritage?
- Do you have young children in the house?

These are just a few of the questions that you should ask yourself in narrowing down the right breed for you. Think about every aspect of your life and consider how your dog should fit in.

Before you get a puppy, like one of these Biewer Terriers, consider if you have the time to dedicate to walks, training, daily maintenance, and more.

Breeders seek to produce litters stamped with unmistakable breed type, consistent soundness, and excellent temperaments, like with these Pomeranian puppies.

Choose Your Breeder

Once you settle on a breed, you come to the next and most important step—finding that perfect puppy. When you start your search, the most often-repeated bit of advice you'll hear is: "Go to a responsible breeder."

Many people, though, don't know how to do that, or even what the term really means. You can't just walk up to a person selling puppies and say, "Are you a responsible breeder?" The answer, of course, will be "YES!"

Before you start looking, you need to understand the real meaning of the words "responsible" or "reputable" breeder and how you can distinguish between that person and someone just out to make a buck, or someone who may be well-meaning but hasn't the time, energy, or experience to breed quality puppies. It is not simply a matter of putting two nice dogs together and hoping for the best.

What Is a Responsible Breeder?

Dog breeding is both science and art. A breeder must know all about canine genetics and anatomy, nutrition, and psychology, both canine and human. He or she must know how to read a pedigree to choose sires and dams who will produce beautiful puppies, healthy and sound in both body and mind. The breeder must know the history of the breed, what role these dogs have played through the years, and how that role may be changing in the modern world. He or she must have what is known as "an eye for a dog," an ability to see which dogs in a litter have the physical attributes to be a great example of a breed. The breeder must have a solid background in training and dog behavior, the knowhow to size up a litter and say which puppy has the mental and emotional makeup to someday become a natural show dog, an agility champ, or a great pet.

It's impossible to pick this up overnight. Decades of dedication and experience, learning what works and doesn't, go into dog breeding. Some of the breeders you meet may have whelped their first litters before you were born. And, if you are going to a new breeder, that person will likely have a mentor, a more experienced breeder who has shared knowledge with the newcomer.

A good, AKC®-affiliated breeder will know all about canine genetics and anatomy, like with this Cavalier King Charles Spaniel and her puppies.

Choose a breeder who cares for their litter and the breed in general. See these Toy Poodle puppies.

The best breeders will be intensely involved in the dog world. You will see them at shows and dog-sport events. They are passionate about their breed and its welfare, from the Best in Show ring to rescue. It is not unusual to find some of the top show breeders devoting hours to helping a member of their canine clan who may have fallen on hard times. Some will drive all night to rescue a dog who somehow wound up in a shelter. They love dogs, and they love their breed, sometimes to a point that might seem odd to a newcomer to this world.

Contact the Parent Club

All AKC®-affiliated national breed clubs, known as parent clubs, maintain lists of member-breeders, people who are active in the club, intensely involved with the breed, and adhere to a strict ethics code, established by the clubs. You can find these breeders by going to the AKC® website (*akc.org*), finding your breed of interest, and then clicking on the link to the national parent club. If you are new to a breed, read through all the information on the site.

Why Register Your Puppy?

You may want to compete with your puppy someday even if dog shows or any other activities may not be on your mind when you buy your puppy. As you live with your dog, that might change. To participate in events, your dog must be AKC®-registered, and AKC® rules require that the dog be registered within twelve months of the date the litter is registered.

Registering your puppy helps all dogs, through such AKC® programs as: kennel inspections, AKC® Canine Health Foundation, AKC® Reunite Pet Disaster Relief Trailers, AKC® Humane Fund, Canine Good Citizen® (CGC), public education, and government relations aimed at fair legislation regarding dogs and the people who love them.

For your registration fee, you receive a complimentary trial pet healthcare plan (in some states), a certificate for a complimentary veterinary office visit, a new puppy handbook, The Pupdate newsletter, and other invaluable educational resources to help you raise your puppy.

Green Light or Red Flag?

So, how can you know whether or not someone offering you a puppy is a responsible breeder? The following is a checklist of green lights, qualities that suggest you are in the hands of someone worthy of that description. We also present red flags that will suggest you should look elsewhere for your new family member.

 **GREEN LIGHT**

- The breeder is affiliated with the AKC®, may be an AKC® Breeder of Merit program participant, and may be connected to the AKC® parent club for the breed.

- The breeder eagerly opens his or her home to you. By visiting, you'll get an idea of how the puppy is being raised, and what the mother is like in both looks and temperament.

- The breeder should be aware of breed-specific genetic tests that may identify inheritable health issues, if any are available.

- A breeder will ask you to fill out a questionnaire, sometimes several pages long, and may insist on a series of conversations, on the phone and face-to-face.

- The breeder can show you pedigree information—AKC® registration documents for the sire, dam, and litter. The words "American Kennel Club®" and the AKC® logo should be clearly visible on these documents.

 **RED FLAG**

- A breeder, unaffiliated with any club or organization, who offers no background on the puppy's parents or grandparents.

- The breeder does not allow you into his or her home or, worse, wants to meet you in a parking lot or some other public place.

- A breeder who will not show you any health-screening results, talk about the health issues encountered, or says he or she does not conduct any health or genetic tests because he or she has "never had a problem."

- A breeder who is only interested in whether you can afford the asking price.

- No papers of any kind are offered, there is a charge for registration papers, or the registration papers are from a registry other than the American Kennel Club®. Look carefully at the application because some alternative registries choose names that are very similar to the AKC®, but they are not the real thing.

One of the incredible bonuses of buying a puppy from an AKC® breeder is that you become part of a huge network, a family of people who, like you, love dogs more than anything on earth.

The Sport of Dogs

The arena grows dark and hushed, spotlights dance, and a deep voice comes over a loudspeaker. "We highly encourage you to cheer on your favorites," he urges the crowd, but the spectators need little prodding. They are already shouting the names of the group winners, jumping to their feet to cheer and applaud as, one by one, the best dogs in the country breeze onto the floor.

Thousands of eyes are on the seven glittering, perfectly groomed dogs and their handlers moving in a graceful circle around the carpeted floor. It is the moment of truth, the selection of the top dog, Best in Show, at a major event.

When people think of the sport of dogs, this is what often comes to mind, and for good reason. Such events have been a part of the American landscape since before there was a Brooklyn Bridge or electric lights, when the Westminster Kennel Club held its first bench show in 1877. Seven years later, the founding of the American Kennel Club® opened the country's great age of the dog show.

In the years since, there's been an explosion of sports for four-footed competitors. Today there is something for everyone. Got a Papillon that flies over the furniture? Try agility. Your retriever hangs on your every word? Try obedience, where being a really good dog is a competitive sport. Got a fuzzy shovel who has turned your garden upside down? Earthdog! A hound who chases anything that moves? Lure coursing! A sheepdog who gathers everyone in the house into one corner? Herding! A Bloodhound who can't get his nose off the ground? Mantrailing or tracking!

AKC® sports and activities fall into five categories: dog shows (conformation), companion events, performance events, the Family Dog Program, and the Title Recognition Program.

Name your dog's passion, and there's an AKC® activity for it. The opportunities for fun and frolic are endless. In the following pages, we'll introduce you to just a few of the many sports and activities AKC® has to offer. For more details on rules, regulations, and titles, visit the AKC® website, *www.akc.org*.

The AKC® National Championship has become one the nation's most prestigious and exciting dog shows, usually attracting the largest entries of the year.

The AKC® National Championship not only offers breed classes for all recognized breeds but also features a junior-handling competition, shown here.

Conformation

The signature event held under AKC® rules is the dog show, also known as a conformation event. Judges evaluate a dog's conformation, which means how the dog's physical structure and temperament compare to the breed standard, the blueprint of an ideal representative.

WHO MAY PARTICIPATE?

For conformation shows, a dog must:
- Be individually registered with the American Kennel Club®
- Be six months of age or older
- Be a breed for which classes are offered at the show
- Be unaltered. Spayed or neutered dogs are not eligible to compete in conformation classes because the purpose of a dog show is to evaluate breeding stock. One exception to this rule is in Junior Showmanship, where spayed and neutered dogs can be shown.

Children of All Ages

One thing that strikes first-timers to an AKC® event is the great range in the ages among the human participants. It is not unusual to see teenage handlers competing against people old enough to be their grandparents. Age in the competitive dog world is truly just a number, and among the great joys of being part of it are the friendships that leap across the generation gap. From nine to ninety, pick up a show lead, and you have something in common.

The AKC®'s Junior Showmanship program is designed to help youngsters gain dog show experience in conformation. These classes are open to juniors from nine to eighteen years old and are aimed at helping young dog lovers develop handling skills and learn about good sportsmanship, dogs, and dog shows. There are additional opportunities for youngsters in companion and performance events. These programs offer young people direction if they are considering careers that involve dogs, along with a solid foundation for a lifetime of loving canine companions.

Agility

"Addictive" is the word most participants use to describe this fast-paced sport, which was launched in England in the late 1970s. It was invented as a kind of a half-time entertainment during the annual Crufts dog show, with obstacles based on equestrian competitions. The popularity of the sport soared after its introduction in the United States in the 1980s.

Agility tests a team's skill at negotiating a complex course composed of jumps, tunnels, and other obstacles. Border Collies, Shetland Sheepdogs, and other herding breeds rule here, but you'll see all kinds, from squat Bulldogs to majestic Great Danes, as well as mixed breeds, dashing around the courses.

Obedience

This is a chance to show off how well you and your dog work together as a team by performing a series of obedience exercises that are scored by a judge. At the most fundamental level, teams are judged on how well they perform the simple commands that every dog should know—sit, down, heel, and stay. You can start with informal matches, held by local dog clubs, and then progress to formal AKC® competitions. There are several levels, each with more advanced skills and challenging exercises.

Tracking

Dogs are geniuses when it comes to following their noses, which are thousands of times more sensitive than those of humans. A puppy instinctively uses his nose—training your dog to track simply hones his natural ability. And since all dogs have a natural ability to follow a scent, any breed is capable of learning to track. Tracking requires very little equipment. You just need a harness, a 20- to- 40-foot lead, a few flags to mark your track, and an open grassy area free of obstacles, such as roads, ditches, or woods.

Agility attracts toy breeds, like the Pomeranian, to its exciting, timed obstacle courses.

AKC Scent Work®

AKC Scent Work® is a sport that mimics the task of working detection dogs—such as drug dogs or explosives dogs—in finding a specific scent and communicating to the handler that the scent has been found. In Scent Work, the dog-handler teams are placed in a search area in which a target odor (such as an essential oil) has been hidden out of sight. Each dog must use nothing but his sense of smell to locate the hide, and the handler must trust when the dog has found it, confidently calling out "alert!" to the judge. Scent-work searches are conducted in a variety of everyday environments; for example, in a scent- work trial, a dog might be asked to find the odor in a collection of luggage, in a classroom, around a baseball dugout, or buried up to 6 inches beneath the ground. All purebred dogs and mixed breeds are eligible to participate in AKC Scent Work®.

AKC Rally®

In rally, dog-and-handler teams negotiate a course of exercises following sequentially numbered signs, known as stations. Each team progresses from sign to sign at its own pace, performing exercises that are written in pictographs on the signs.

The Papillon, shown here, is great at agility courses.

Unlike obedience, where commands may be given only once and handlers may not verbally encourage their dogs, in rally it is fine to praise the dog throughout your run. Judges score the teams on how accurately they perform the exercises and how well they work together.

Fast CAT®

The Fast CAT® event presents dogs with a straight-line 100-yard dash. The dog's time is converted to miles per hour (mph), and they earn points based on their mph to earn titles. The best of the best are showcased on the AKC® website, which ranks the top twenty fastest dogs by breed.

Canine Good Citizen®/AKC S.T.A.R. Puppy®

Every dog, mixed or purebred, can earn the Canine Good Citizen® (CGC) title, demonstrating that he has the manners and skills to live in polite society. Since the CGC program began, more than one million dogs have earned the CGC award. The CGC test consists of ten items. Some, like accepting a friendly stranger and walking through a crowd, are simply benchmarks of good manners. Other items test basic skills, such as sit, down, stay, and come when called. Once dogs pass the CGC, they can move on for a more advanced title, AKC® Community Canine (CGCA). Dogs also have an opportunity to earn the AKC® Urban CGCTM (CGCU) title if they can pass a test with challenges unique to a city environment.

The S.T.A.R. Puppy® Program sets a youngster up for success in later activities by providing the basics for a good dog. S.T.A.R. stands for "Socialization, Training, Activity, and a Responsible Owner," which are the cornerstones for a happy, well-behaved pup.

Search and Rescue Title

The Search and Rescue (SAR) title recognizes Federal Emergency Management Agency (FEMA) and state deployable urban SAR dogs. The title may be added to a dog's name and pedigree to designate his SAR skills and accomplishments. Owners are required to also submit a copy of the certificate the dog received from FEMA or the state organization to verify the dog's certification. AKC® has also extended the program to Wilderness SAR dogs. For Wilderness SAR dogs, documentation of at least five actual deployments must be submitted to earn the title.

This Toy Poodle is sprinting in the Fast CAT®.

The Toy Group

Toy breeds may be small in stature, but they have big personalities. These breeds are loving, friendly, and adaptable to various lifestyles. Don't be deceived by their size and charming looks: they are intelligent, energetic, and many possess strong protective instincts.

The tiny breeds of the toy group offer a variety of coat types and colors to suit almost any taste, yet all are small enough to comfortably sit on their owners' laps. Toy dogs excel at being attentive, loving companions. These breeds are especially popular with city dwellers, as their compact size makes them ideal for smaller yards or apartments.

Some of the most popular toy breeds include the Pug, the Shih Tzu, the Pomeranian, the Chuhuahua, and the Yorkshire Terrier. Audrey Hepburn even had a beloved Yorkshire Terrier named Mr. Famous. This adorable pup even made a cameo appearance in Hepburn's film *Funny Face*! It's no doubt that if you choose a toy breed, you will have a lovable companion for life.

The Maltese is a great companion dog.

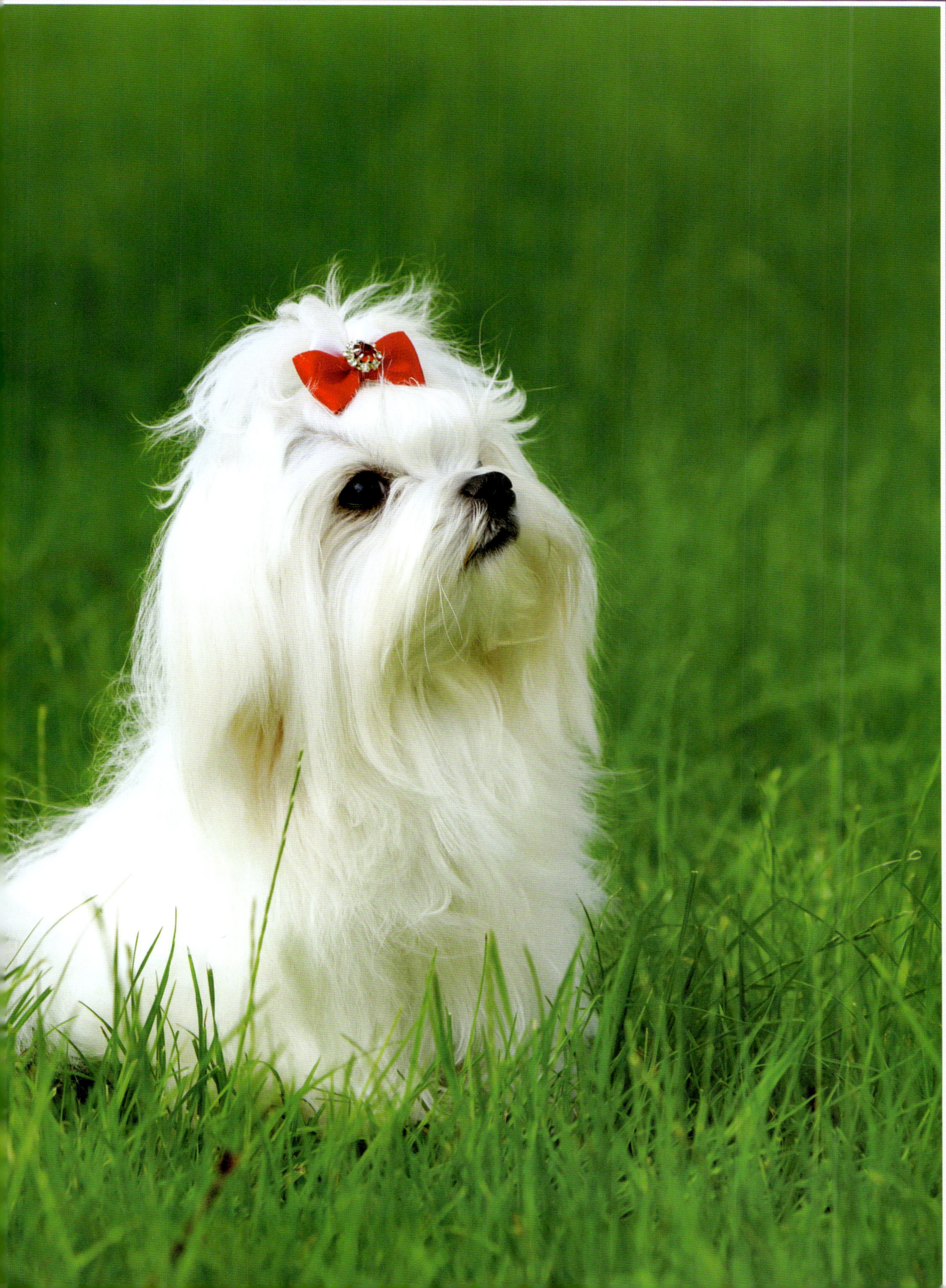

Meet the Affenpinscher

Recognized by AKC® in 1936
Affenpinscher Club of America (affenpinscher.org), formed in 1965

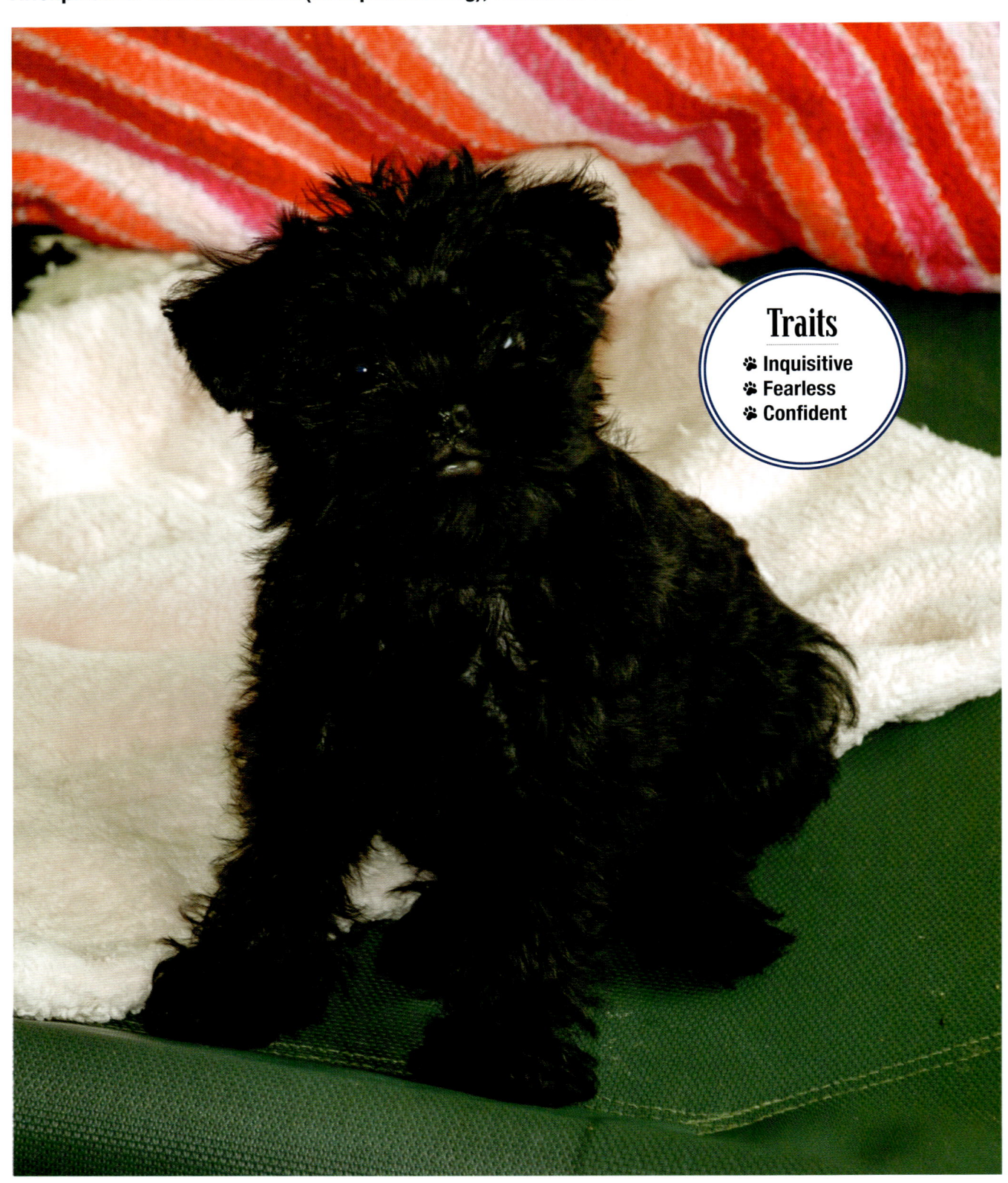

Traits
- Inquisitive
- Fearless
- Confident

HISTORY

One of the oldest of toy dogs, the Affenpinscher (translated from German as "monkey-like terrier") originated in Central Europe. Affenpinschers appear in artwork dating back to the fifteenth century. During the seventeenth century, small terriers frequently were kept around stables on farms or in stores where they served as ratters. Bred down in size, these small terriers evolved to become the Affenpinscher, while their larger prototype developed into the Schnauzer. Accepted as indoor companions, Affens kept mice from overrunning the home. Early breeders of the Affenpinscher and Schnauzer did much crossing between the two and with select other breeds to develop the type they were seeking in each breed. These crosses were responsible for the coat color and type that appear in the Affenpinscher today. In France, where the breed became extremely popular, they were nicknamed Diablotin Moustachu, or "mustached little devil."

Two Affenpinschers were imported to the United States in the spring of 1935, one of which had been bred prior to importation and thereby whelped the first Affen litter in the States. Affenpinschers were first listed in the AKC® Stud Book in November 1936. A minimal number of litters was bred following that, and none between 1940 and 1949. The early 1950s was a period of rebuilding, as the initial imports had died out. In 1966, one year after the founding of the Affenpinscher Club of America, the breed received some much-needed publicity when This Week magazine featured an Affen pup on its cover. Since then, they have charmed their way into many American homes and, despite their small numbers, have great success in the show ring. The breed received another huge boost at the 2013 Westminster Kennel Club dog show when an Affenpinscher named GCh. Banana Joe v Tani Kazari took Best in Show.

FORM AND FUNCTION

A game, alert, intelligent, and sturdy little terrier type, the Affenpinscher is characterized by his monkey-like expression, derived from his prominent chin and pouting lower lip, open nostrils, and mustache. This expression is further accentuated by his bushy eyebrows and large, round, dark eyes framed with hair that stands off from the head. Sound physical structure allows him to walk on his back legs in parody of the organ grinder's monkey, and the "neat but shaggy" appearance of his short, harsh-textured coat enhances that mimicry. His innate intelligence leads him into monkey mischief on a daily basis. The boldness of his "big dog in a small body" attitude is demonstrated by the Affen's protectiveness regarding his owner, his home, and his possessions. Most Affens retain their terrier-inherited prey drive and are still willing and able to rid the house of vermin.

LIVING WITH AN AFFEN

When choosing a puppy, size and a square outline are important for type. Some Affenpinschers are larger, but this is a toy dog and small size is important. Affens are comfortable in the city or the country, in apartments or mansions, but are definitely not suitable as merely a yard ornament. They require constant interaction with their humans to be happy, well-adjusted pets. Affenpinschers are very portable and, with their owners, love being in the cabin of a plane, in the car or RV, or in a tote bag, helping with daily errands.

Intelligent and inquisitive, but inclined to think independently, they have an eagerness to please that makes them highly trainable. Be prepared to train with positive reinforcement of desired behavior and immediate correction of bad behavior. Their fearless attitude, an endearing feature of the breed, must be supervised in the company of larger dogs. If the Affen is to be left alone during the day, a securely penned area is suggested, as their inquisitive attitude can get them into mischief when not supervised.

COMPETITION

The versatile Affenpinscher is capable of successfully competing not only in conformation but also in obedience, rally, and agility. With terriers as their forebears, Affens are inclined to think independently but are eager to please and respond well to positive reinforcement.

Official Standard for the Affenpinscher

General Appearance: The Affenpinscher is a balanced, wiry-haired terrier-like toy dog whose intelligence and demeanor make it a good house pet. Originating in Germany, the name Affenpinscher means "monkey-like terrier." The breed was developed to rid the kitchens, granaries, and stables of rodents. In France the breed is described as the "Diablotin Moustachu" or moustached little devil. Both describe the appearance and attitude of this delightful breed. The total overall appearance of the Affenpinscher is more important than any individual characteristic. He is described as having a neat but shaggy appearance.

Size, Proportion, Substance: A sturdy, compact dog with medium bone, not delicate in any way. Preferred height at the withers is 9½ to 11½ inches. Withers height is approximately the same as the length of the body from the point of the shoulder to point of the buttocks, giving a square appearance. The female may be slightly longer.

Head: The head is in proportion to the body, carried confidently with monkey-like facial expression. *Eyes*—Round, dark, brilliant, and of medium size in proportion to the head but not bulging or protruding. Eye rims are black. *Ears*—Cropped to a point, set high and standing erect; or natural, standing erect, semi-erect or dropped. All of the above types of ears, if symmetrical, are acceptable as long as the monkey-like expression is maintained. *Skull*—Round and domed, but not coarse. *Stop*—Well-defined. *Muzzle*—Short and narrowing slightly to a blunt nose. The length of the muzzle is approximately the same as the distance between the eyes. *Nose*—Black, turned neither up nor down. *Lips*—Black, with prominent lower lip. *Bite*—Slightly undershot. A level bite is acceptable if the monkey-like expression is maintained. An overshot bite is to be severely penalized. A wry mouth is a serious fault. The teeth and tongue do not show when the mouth is closed. The lower jaw is broad enough for the lower teeth to be straight and even.

Neck, Topline, Body: *Neck*—Short and straight. *Topline*—Straight and level. *Body*—The *chest* is moderately broad and deep; ribs are moderately sprung. Tuckup is slight. The *back* is short and level with a strong loin. The *croup* has just a perceptible curve. Tail may be docked or natural. A docked tail is generally between 1 and 2 inches long, set high and carried erect. The natural tail is set high and carried curved gently up over the back while moving. The type of tail is not a major consideration.

Forequarters: Front angulation is moderate. *Shoulders*—With moderate layback. The length of the shoulder blade and the upper arm are about equal. *Elbows*—Close to the body. *Front legs* straight when viewed from any direction. *Pasterns* short and straight. *Dewclaws* generally removed. *Feet* small, round, and compact with black pads and nails.

Hindquarters: Rear angulation is moderate to match the front. *Hindlegs*—Straight when viewed from behind. From the side, hindlegs are set under the body to maintain a square appearance. The length of the upper thigh and the second thigh are about equal with moderate bend to the stifle. *Hocks*—Moderately angulated.

Coat: Dense hair, rough, harsh, and about 1 inch in length on the shoulders and body. May be shorter on the rear and tail. Head, neck, chest, stomach and legs have longer, less harsh coat. The mature Affenpinscher has a mane or cape of strong hair which blends into the back coat at the withers area. The longer hair on the head, eyebrows and beard stands off and frames the face to emphasize the monkey-like expression. Hair on the ears is cut very short. A correct coat needs little grooming to blend the various lengths of hair to maintain a neat but shaggy appearance.

Color: Black, gray, silver, red, black and tan, or belge are all acceptable. Blacks may have a rusty cast or a few white or silver hairs mixed with the black. Reds may vary from a brownish red to an orangey tan. Belge has black, brown, and/or white hairs mixed with the red. With various colors, the furnishings may be a bit lighter. Some dogs may have black masks. A small white spot on the chest is not penalized, but large white patches are undesirable. Color is not a major consideration.

Gait: Light, free, sound, balanced, confident, the Affenpinscher carries itself with comic seriousness. Viewed from the front or rear, while walking, the legs move parallel to each other. Trotting, the feet will converge toward a midline as speed increases. Unsound gait is to be heavily penalized.

Temperament: General demeanor is game, alert, and inquisitive with great loyalty and affection toward its master and friends. The breed is generally quiet, but can become vehemently excited when threatened or attacked, and is fearless toward any aggressor.

Approved June 12, 2000
Effective July 27, 2000

Meet the Biewer Terrier

Recognized by AKC® in 2021
Biewer Terrier Club of America (biewerterrierclubofamerica.org), formed in 2006

Traits
- Whimsical
- Devoted
- Fun-Loving

HISTORY

The Biewer Terrier originated in Germany, in 1984, when two tricolor puppies were born in the kennel of experienced Yorkshire Terrier breeders Werner and Gertrude Biewer. A veterinarian friend suggested they call the dogs Biewer Yorkshire Terriers. Soon afterward a famous German singer took a liking to the dogs, adding the words "a la Pom Pon" to the breed name. In the following years, the Biewers continued to work on developing a consistent population of the charming little dogs through selective breedings.

American dog fanciers began importing the breed from Germany beginning in 2002. The delightful dogs quickly caught on in the US, with clubs forming as early as 2006 to protect and promote the new breed. During this period, the Biewer Terrier Club of America was formed.

The BTCA contacted Mars Veterinary in early 2007 to see if the lab could develop a program to confirm whether the Biewer Terrier was in fact a strain of the Yorkshire Terrier or a separate breed. By September 2007, the lab was ready with DNA testing for this purpose, and BTCA members submitted a number of blood samples to begin the work. The results of these tests showed the samples clustered together in a way typical of a pure breed, but separate from the Yorkshire Terrier. These new results prompted the submission of further, more varied samples. This would be the first time a breed was confirmed to be pure through the collection of genetic material, rather than through pedigree records.

This whimsical little toy breed is *wunderbar*, as Mrs. Biewer herself said when two BTCA members visited her in Germany in 2007. The BTCA founding members worked long and hard to protect and perfect the breed, now named Biewer Terrier. After years of diligent work by the BTCA, the breed was accepted into the AKC's Foundation Stock Service® in 2014 and achieved full recognition as a member of the Toy Group as of January 2021.

FORM AND FUNCTION

The characteristics of the Biewer (pronounced BEE-ver) Terrier contribute toward his being a charming, delightful pet and companion. The standard describes the breed as having a "whimsical, childlike attitude." At just four to eight pounds, these tiny dogs can go with their owners almost anywhere, and with their fun-loving, friendly demeanor, they quickly make friends with everyone they meet.

LIVING WITH A BIEWER TERRIER

Biewer Terriers are loyal and devoted to their family. They're also smart and love to solve problems and learn new things. Training should begin as soon as the new puppy is brought home and should always be gentle and upbeat, with happy rewards such as treats or praise. Socialization, which a is must for every dog, entails non-intimidating, fun exposure to a wide variety of people, places, and experiences—this will help ensure the pup matures into a confident, well-adjusted adult dog who is happy and secure in a variety of settings.

Most owners can care for the Biewer's coat themselves if they wish to. A short "puppy cut" can make maintenance easy. If kept long, the Biewer's beautiful soft, silky coat needs daily brushing. A tip from breeders is to brush the coat with a spritz of water mixed with conditioner (made for dogs) misted over it, rather than brushing while dry. This helps reduce damage to the coat. Bathing once a week can keep the dog clean; for males, a quick daily cleaning of the underbelly area with a wet cloth keeps this area fresh. If using a hair dryer with these little dogs, remember that their skin is very delicate and easily burned. As for all dogs, and toy-breed dogs especially, attention to care of the teeth should begin from a young age and continue throughout the dog's life.

COMPETITION

The Biewer Terrier is intelligent, lively, and eager to please. In addition to conformation competition at dog shows, the breed excels in the many companion events offered by AKC®, including obedience, rally, tracking, and agility, and can be an energetic participant in activities such as Trick Dog™, Scent Work, and more.

Official Standard for the Biewer Terrier

General Appearance: The Biewer Terrier is an elegant, longhaired, uniquely colored toy terrier with a breed signature ponytail. The coat parts down the middle, hanging straight and evenly on both sides of the body as though a comb has been used to part it. The back is level, with height at withers being equal to height at the croup. Although the outline of the dog gives the appearance of a square, the body length is slightly longer than the overall height. The tail is set high and carried well arched over the body, covered with a long luxurious plume. The Biewer Terrier has a lighthearted whimsical, childlike attitude. Although mischievous at times, they are obedient and make a loyal companion.

Size, Proportion, Substance: *Size*—Height at the withers is the same as the height at the croup, measuring 7 to 11 inches, with weight being 4 to 8 pounds. *Proportion*—Length of body from prosternum to ischium is longer than overall height, making the dog off square although square is acceptable. *Substance*—Body is fine to medium boned with a level top line. Serious fault—Over 8 pounds.

Head: *Expression*—Is more human than that of a dog, being bright and intelligent. *Eyes*—Are medium sized and may be round or almond shaped with a crisp, clear countenance. *Iris*—as dark as possible. *Ears*—Are small, upright, V shaped, moderately wide set and covered with hair except the tips being shaved. They are set to the back of the skull and the base is level with the eyes. *Skull*—Slightly rounded. Stop—Moderate. *Muzzle*—One-third the length of the head.

Eye rims, Nose, and Lips: Completely black. *Bite*—Level or scissor bite. Teeth—Straight and even. Serious fault—Incomplete pigment on the eye rims, nose, and lip; ears not standing erect. Disqualifications—Blue eye(s); Brown or liver pigmentation of the eye rims, nose, and lips.

Neck, Topline and Body: *Neck*—Moderate in length, free from throatiness. *Topline*—Level. *Body*—Length is slightly longer than the overall height although square is acceptable. Chest—Comes to the elbows with a good width. Ribs—Moderately sprung. Underline—Slightly tucked up. Back—Level topline. Loin—Well developed and strong. *Tail*—Set high when in movement carried well arched over the body in a graceful sickle curve, covered with a long luxurious plume. Plume lies to either side of the body. Length of tailbone must go to the stifles or longer. When reposed, the tail may be relaxed. A kink in the tail is not to be faulted. Serious faults—Roach or rounded back; high in the front or rear.

Forequarters: Forelegs should be straight, elbows neither in nor out. Angulation—Moderate. Shoulders are nicely laid back to allow for good reach and freedom of movement. Elbows—Set close to the body. Legs—Straight when viewed from the front are muscular and covered with hair. Pasterns—Up and straight. Dewclaws—May be removed but not required. Feet—Round. Toes—Well arched covered with hair which may be trimmed not to impede movement or trimmed to show the shape of the foot. Pads—Black and/or flesh. Nails—Black and/or white. Disqualification—Brown or liver pigmentation of the pads.

Hindquarters: In balance with the forequarters. Angulation—Rear to match front. Legs—Hind legs are straight when viewed from behind, muscular and covered with hair. Stifle— Slightly bent when viewed from the side. Hocks—Straight when viewed from behind, pointing neither in nor out. Dewclaws—May be removed but not required. Feet—Round. Toes—Well arched covered with hair which may be trimmed not to impede movement or trimmed to show the shape of the foot. Pads—Black and/or flesh. Nails—Black and/or white. Disqualification—Brown or liver pigmentation of the pads.

Coat: Long and flowing with a soft silky texture. Hair is straight without an undercoat, hanging close to the ground if not touching. Coat may be trimmed to floor length for ease of movement. Head fall is tied up into a single ponytail on top of the head, hanging loose. Puppy ponytails may be placed a little lower on the head as to gather the short hairs. A bow is used for adornment; no topknots or rollovers. Feet are trimmed for a neat, clean appearance. Trim around anus. *Head falls that display topknots or roll overs common to other breeds shall be so severely penalized as to be eliminated from competition.*

Color: The Biewer Terrier is a uniquely colored toy terrier. Head Coloring—Blue/Black, Gold/Tan and White in good symmetry. Any combination of the following two colors, (Blue/Black and Gold/Tan); (Gold/Tan and White) in good symmetry is acceptable. Body Coloring—Hair on back is blue/black and white. Amounts of each color are of personal preference with no dominating patterns. No amount of tan hair may be found on the back, belly, chest, legs or feet. A small amount of tan hair may be found around the anus. Chest, Stomach, Legs and Tip of the Tail—White. The white from the chest should come up the neck to cover the chin. Legs are to be white from the elbows and stifles to the feet. Disqualification—any other color or combination of colors other than those that are listed.

Gait: The Biewer Terrier moves with confidence and pride. Movement should be graceful, smooth and straightforward without being stilted or hackneyed. When viewed from the side the top line remains level, he gives an impression of rapid movement, size considered. Hind legs should track in line with the front legs, going neither inside nor outside. Tail must be up when in movement. Serious Fault—Hackneyed gait in adults.

Temperament: Intelligent, loyal and very devoted to their human family. They have a fun loving, childlike attitude that makes them a great companion for all ages. They quickly make friends with animals of any origin.

The foregoing description is of the ideal Biewer Terrier. Any deviation from the above described dog must be penalized to the extent of the deviation.

Serious Faults: Over 8 pounds; Incomplete pigment on the eye rims, nose, and lips; ears not standing erect; Roach or rounded back; high in front or rear; Hackneyed gait in adults.

Eliminating Faults: Head falls that display topknots or roll overs common to other breeds.

Disqualifications:
Blue eye(s); Brown or liver pigmentation of the eye rims, nose, lips and pads. Any other color or combination of colors other than those that are listed.

Effective July 3, 2019

Meet the Brussels Griffon

Recognized by AKC® in 1900
American Brussels Griffon Association (www.abga.club), formed in 1945

Traits
- Highly Intelligent
- Alert
- Sensitive

AKC Official Guide to Toy Dogs

Brussels Griffon

HISTORY

As early as the fifteenth century, small wire-coated dogs existed in many parts of Europe. These self-reliant characters were widely used as ratters in stables, outbuildings, and anywhere quantities of grain were stored. This terrier-type Brussels Griffon forebear was a little larger than today's breed, with a longer foreface that more closely resembled the Affenpinscher. Although there is no complete record of the breeds crossed and re-crossed with this early little terrier to create today's Brussels Griffon, it is accepted by the American Brussels Griffon Association that the Pug and the English Toy Spaniel were of the strongest influence in creating the Brussels Griffon we know today.

The Brussels Griffon was known in its present form on the European continent by 1870. This "now flat-faced" cobby little dog, having moved from the stables to the ladies' sitting rooms, became quite the rage among the wealthy and a favorite of artists in the early 1870s. The Belgian royal family's infatuation with the breed dates back to 1894. In 1899, Brussels Griffons were first listed in the AKC® Stud Book and shown at the Westminster Kennel Club in the Miscellaneous Class. In 1900, the breed gained its own classification, and the first AKC® champion was recorded in 1908. Shortly after World War I, the first Brussels Griffon specialty was held in New York City with an entry of fifty-three. From these early dates to the present time, this clever little trickster has wormed his way into the hearts and homes of all susceptible to his many charms.

FORM AND FUNCTION

Small but sturdy, the square body of a Griffon, weighing about 8 to 10 pounds, should be a "picture of substance, not elegance." His Griffon pout, created by the placement of eyes and nose and the upswept jaw, gives these toy dogs near human expression.

LIVING WITH A GRIFFON

An ideal owner for the Brussels Griffon is someone who places a high priority on companionship and the safety of the dog, has a generous sense of humor, and is able to enjoy this highly intelligent little scamp's attempts to pull one over at every turn and still offer him a lap for the evening when it is time to snuggle. This breed generally has a lengthy life and is meant to live with and enjoy nearly every aspect of being part of its family. If Griffons are shut away from the family's center, they will pine from a broken heart. A stronger terrier influence in some bloodlines may limit a puppy from being suitable for a young child or the aged, while a more laid-back puppy might be ideal in either role. The health, appearance, and behavior of the new puppy will largely reflect how well you do your homework when choosing a breeder.

This is a very clever breed that thrives in an environment of interaction and training. If left to their own devices, Griffons can become destructive from boredom. The breed comes in both a rough and a smooth coat with the following colors allowed to be shown: red, belge (a mixture of black and reddish brown), black and tan, and solid black. The smooth-coated variety requires very little care other than seasonal raking of the undercoat. The rough-coated variety must be hand-stripped to keep tidy and relieve the coat of loose hairs or, if not being shown, he can be put in a Schnauzer clip (minus the eyebrows).

COMPETITION

Today's Brussels Griffon has much success in conformation, obedience, rally, and agility.

Official Standard for the Brussels Griffon

General Appearance: A toy dog, intelligent, alert, sturdy, with a thickset, short body, a smart carriage and set-up, attracting attention by an almost human expression. There are two distinct types of coat: rough or smooth. Except for coat, there is no difference between the two.

Size, Proportion, Substance: *Size*—Weight usually 8 to 10 pounds, and should not exceed 12 pounds. Type and quality are of greater importance than weight, and a smaller dog that is sturdy and well proportioned should not be penalized. *Proportion*—Square, as measured from point of shoulder to rearmost projection of upper thigh and from withers to ground. *Substance*—Thickset, compact with good balance. Well boned.

Head: A very important feature. An almost human *expression*. *Eyes* set well apart, very large, black, prominent, and well open. The eyelashes long and black. Eyelids edged with black. *Ears* small and set rather high on the head. May be shown cropped or natural. If natural they are carried semi-erect. *Skull* large and round, with a domed forehead. The stop deep. *Nose* very black, extremely short, its tip being set back deeply between the eyes so as to form a lay-back. The nostrils large. *Disqualifications*—Dudley or butterfly nose. *Lips* edged with black, not pendulous but well brought together, giving a clean finish to the mouth. *Jaws* must be undershot. The incisors of the lower jaw should protrude over the upper incisors. The lower jaw is prominent, rather broad with an upward sweep. Neither teeth nor tongue should show when the mouth is closed. A wry mouth is a serious fault. *Disqualifications*—Bite overshot. Hanging tongue.

Neck, Topline, Body: *Neck* medium length, gracefully arched. *Topline*—Back level and short. *Body*—A thickset, short body. Brisket should be broad and deep, ribs well sprung. Short-coupled. *Tail*—Set and held high, docked to about one-third.

Forequarters: Forelegs medium length, straight in bone, well muscled, set moderately wide apart and straight from the point of the shoulders as viewed from the front. Pasterns short and strong. Feet round, small, and compact, turned neither in nor out. Toes well arched. Black pads and toenails preferred.

Hindquarters: Hind legs set true, thighs strong and well muscled, stifles bent, hocks well let down, turning neither in nor out.

Coat: The *rough coat* is wiry and dense, the harder and more wiry the better. On no account should

Scale of Points

Head
Skull	5
Nose and stop	10
Eyes	5
Bite, chin and jaw	10
Ears	5
Subtotal	**35**

Coat
Color	12
Texture	13
Subtotal	**25**

Body and General Conformation
Body (brisket and rib)	15
Gait	10
Legs and feet	5
General appearance (neck, topline and tail carriage)	10
Subtotal	**40**
Total	**100**

---

the dog look or feel woolly, and there should be no silky hair anywhere. The coat should not be so long as to give a shaggy appearance, but should be distinctly different all over from the smooth coat. The head should be covered with wiry hair, slightly longer around the eyes, nose, cheeks, and chin, thus forming a fringe. The rough coat is hand-stripped and should never appear unkempt. Body coat of sufficient length to determine texture. The coat may be tidied for neatness of appearance, but coats prepared with scissors and/or clippers should be severely penalized. The *smooth coat* is straight, short, tight and glossy, with no trace of wiry hair.

Color: Either 1) *Red:* reddish brown with a little black at the whiskers and chin allowable; 2) *Belge:* black and reddish brown mixed, usually with black mask and whiskers; 3) *Black and Tan:* black with uniform reddish brown markings, appearing under the chin, on the legs, above each eye, around the edges of the ears and around the vent; or 4) *Black:* solid black.

Any white hairs are a serious fault, except for "frost" on the muzzle of a mature dog, which is natural. *Disqualification*—White spot or blaze anywhere on coat.

Gait: Movement is a straightforward, purposeful trot, showing moderate reach and drive, and maintaining a steady topline.

Temperament: Intelligent, alert and sensitive. Full of self-importance.

Disqualifications: Dudley or butterfly nose. Bite overshot. Hanging tongue. White spot or blaze anywhere on coat.

Approved November 8, 2022
Effective February 1, 2023

Meet the Cavalier King Charles Spaniel

Recognized by AKC® in 1995
American Cavalier King Charles Spaniel Club (ackcsc.org), formed in 1994

Traits
- Friendly
- Graceful
- Gentle

HISTORY

Toy spaniels, a part of European court life as early as the fifteenth century, were sometimes referred to as "comforter spaniels" because they snuggled in their owner's laps. They were immortalized in the art of such famous painters as Van Dyck, Titian, Landseer, and Stubbs, but their association with the royalty of England has irrevocably linked them to "that sceptered isle." Mary Queen of Scots, Charles I and Charles II, and later the Duke and Duchess of Marlborough, all helped to popularize these charming little dogs. Charles II was particularly enamored of them, so much so that they became forever identified with his name. Although the Cavalier's popularity was eventually supplanted by the shorter muzzled, domeheaded King Charles Spaniel (a related but separate breed), an American by the name of Roswell Eldridge became intrigued by the old Cavalier type and offered a substantial reward at the 1926 Crufts Dog Show in England for winners of Cavalier classes. From that time to the present, the future of the breed has never been in doubt. Today, the Cavalier is the most popular toy dog in England. The first Cavaliers were sent to the United States in 1952, but it was not until 1996 that the Cavalier achieved full recognition by the AKC®. The American Cavalier King Charles Spaniel Club was incorporated in 1994. Today, the Cavalier ranks among the AKC®'s top twenty-five breeds.

FORM AND FUNCTION

The Cavalier was never designed to be anything other than a sweet, gentle lapdog, to please the ladies of the royal court. He was developed to have a soft, gentle expression and a glamorous coat, to be all the more attractive to his owners who loved to gaze down into his large, limpid eyes. In the eighteenth century, John Churchill, the Duke of Marlborough, became a great patron of the Blenheim color (red and white) and demanded that his Blenheims be hardy and "able to go all day behind a horse." All four colors were eventually bred to be sound as well as beautiful, and Cavaliers are small, glamorous, but sturdy dogs of considerable endurance. At the same time, at ideal weights of only 13 to 18 pounds, they can be picked up and handled with ease. Because the royals often had a number of these dogs living in the palace confines, they were bred to be congenial with each other, and they remain very dog-tolerant today.

LIVING WITH A CAVALIER

Cavaliers are not fast developers as baby puppies and often do not go to new homes before ten to twelve weeks of age. At that tender age, it is very difficult to select a show prospect, as the breed is notorious for changing dramatically in physical appearance until maturity. New owners choosing a pet puppy should look for a bright, happy pup who is engaging, interacts well with people, and appears sound and healthy. Attractive markings are the proverbial icing on the cake.

The Cavalier does not demand more than a loving home…and a fenced yard. Cavaliers are not reliable to obey commands if they are busy chasing butterflies or birds, so a good fence is a must. And they must be protected from larger and more aggressive dogs. Well-behaved children are happy companions, but parents must be careful that the kids are not too rough on their small charges. The Cavalier's silky coat is kept natural and untrimmed but needs regular brushing and occasional bathing to keep it mat- and tangle-free. In general, Cavaliers are very fond of cats, although the reverse is not always true! Most Cavaliers remain very healthy dogs into old age, often living into their teen years.

COMPETITION

Many Cavaliers excel in agility and make grand obedience dogs. They are very competitive in the conformation ring, and they are marvelous therapy dogs. Although eager to please, they are not always the easiest to train, as their attention span is sometimes easily diverted.

Official Standard for the Cavalier King Charles Spaniel

General Appearance: The Cavalier King Charles Spaniel is an active, graceful, well-balanced toy spaniel, very gay and free in action; fearless and sporting in character, yet at the same time gentle and affectionate. It is this typical gay temperament, combined with true elegance and royal appearance which are of paramount importance in the breed. Natural appearance with no trimming, sculpting or artificial alteration is essential to breed type.

Size, Proportion, Substance: *Size*—Height 12 to 13 inches at the withers; weight proportionate to height, between 13 and 18 pounds. A small, well balanced dog within these weights is desirable, but these are ideal heights and weights and slight variations are permissible. *Proportion*—The body approaches squareness, yet, if measured from point of shoulder to point of buttock, is slightly longer than the height at the withers. The height from the withers to the elbow is approximately equal to the height from the elbow to the ground. *Substance*—Bone moderate in proportion to size. Weedy and coarse specimens are to be equally penalized.

Head: Proportionate to size of dog, appearing neither too large nor too small for the body. Expression—The sweet, gentle, melting expression is an important breed characteristic. Eyes—Large, round, but not prominent and set well apart; color a warm, very dark brown; giving a lustrous, limpid look. Rims dark. There should be cushioning under the eyes which contributes to the soft expression. Faults—Small, almond-shaped, prominent, or light eyes; white surrounding ring. Ears—Set high, but not close, on top of the head. Leather long with plenty of feathering and wide enough so that when the dog is alert, the ears fan slightly forward to frame the face. Skull—Slightly rounded, but without dome or peak; it should appear flat because of the high placement of the ears. Stop is moderate, neither filled nor deep. Muzzle—Full muzzle slightly tapered. Length from base of stop to tip of nose about 1½ inches. Face well filled below eyes. Any tendency towards snipiness undesirable. Nose pigment uniformly black without flesh marks and nostrils well developed. Lips well developed but not pendulous giving a clean finish. Faults—Sharp or pointed muzzles. Bite—A perfect, regular and complete scissors bite is preferred, i.e., the upper teeth closely overlapping the lower teeth and set square into the jaws. Faults—Undershot bite, weak or crooked teeth, crooked jaws.

Neck, Topline, Body: *Neck*—Fairly long, without throatiness, well enough muscled to form a slight arch at the crest. Set smoothly into nicely sloping shoulders to give an elegant look. *Topline*—Level both when moving and standing. *Body*—Short-coupled with ribs well sprung but not barrelled. Chest moderately deep, extending to elbows allowing ample heart room. Slightly less body at the flank than at the last rib, but with no tucked-up appearance. Tail—Well set on, carried happily but never much above the level of the back, and in constant characteristic motion when the dog is in action. Docking is optional. If docked, no more than one-third to be removed.

Forequarters: Shoulders well laid back. Forelegs straight and well under the dog with elbows close to the sides. Pasterns strong and feet compact with well-cushioned pads. Dewclaws may be removed.

Hindquarters: The hindquarters construction should come down from a good broad pelvis, moderately muscled; stifles well turned and hocks well let down. The hindlegs when viewed from the rear should parallel each other from hock to heel. Faults—Cow or sickle hocks.

Coat: Of moderate length, silky, free from curl. Slight wave permissible. Feathering on ears, chest, legs and tail should be long, and the feathering on the feet is a feature of the breed. No trimming of the dog is permitted. Specimens where the coat has been altered by trimming, clipping, or by artificial means shall be so severely penalized as to be effectively eliminated from competition. Hair growing between the pads on the underside of the feet may be trimmed.

Color: There shall be four allowed colors for the Cavalier King Charles Spaniel. *Blenheim*—Rich chestnut markings well broken up on a clear, pearly white ground. The ears must be chestnut and the color evenly spaced on the head and surrounding both eyes, with a white blaze between the eyes and ears, in the center of which may be the lozenge or "Blenheim spot." The lozenge is a unique and desirable, though not essential, characteristic of the Blenheim. *Tricolor*—Jet black markings well broken up on a clear, pearly white ground. The ears must be black and the color evenly spaced on the head and surrounding both eyes, with a white blaze between the eyes. Rich tan markings over the eyes, on cheeks, inside ears and on underside of tail. *Ruby*—Whole-colored rich red. Black and Tan—Jet black with rich, bright tan markings over eyes, on cheeks, inside ears, on chest, legs, and on underside of the tail. Faults—Heavy ticking on Blenheims or Tricolors, white marks on Rubies or Black and Tans. Dogs not of an allowed color shall be disqualified.

Gait: Free moving and elegant in action, with good reach in front and sound, driving rear action. When viewed from the side, the movement exhibits a good length of stride, and viewed from front and rear it is straight and true, resulting from straight-boned fronts and properly made and muscled hindquarters.

Temperament: Gay, friendly, non-aggressive with no tendency towards nervousness or shyness. Bad temper, shyness, and meanness are not to be tolerated and are to be severely penalized as to effectively remove the specimen from competition.

Disqualifications: Dogs not of an allowed color.

Approved January 10, 2023
Effective March 29, 2023

Meet the Chihuahua

Recognized by AKC® in 1904
Chihuahua Club of America (chihuahuaclubofamerica.com), formed in 1923

Traits
- Confident
- Sassy
- Charming

HISTORY

Images of this ancient breed have been found in many parts of the world at different times. It is in the Americas, however, that today's modern Chihuahua is thought to have originated. The Toltec in Mexico had a breed called the Techichi. Carvings of the Techichi from that period closely resemble today's Chihuahua. When the Aztecs conquered the Toltec in the twelfth century, they brought with them a small hairless breed. Some scholars theorize that the modern Chihuahua is a product of the crossbreeding of these two early breeds.

The Chihuahua's history in the United States began in the mid-1800s, with the importation of dogs from Mexico, many from the State of Chihuahua, hence the breed name. In the late 1800s, the first Chihuahua was exhibited at a dog show in Philadelphia. The AKC® recognized the breed in 1904, and the following year a Chihuahua named Beppie was awarded the breed's first conformation championship. In 1952, the AKC® recognized the Long Coat Chihuahua.

Since those early days, the Chihuahua, in both the Long and Smooth Coat varieties, has consistently ranked high in popularity in the United States and around the world.

FORM AND FUNCTION

From its earliest days, the Chihuahua was the companion of Aztec nobles and is thought to have played roles in their religious practices. Today's Chihuahua is a companion dog. With his terrier-like temperament, swiftness of movement, alertness, and intelligence, he makes an adoring addition to any household. His small size and relative hardiness allow him to do well in both city and rural environs.

LIVING WITH A CHIHUAHUA

A Chihuahua's life span can be up to twenty years, so careful selection of your puppy is important for years of enjoyment and companionship. The Chihuahua standard says that the breed's general appearance is of "a graceful, alert, swift-moving, little dog with saucy expression, compact, and with terrier-like qualities of temperament." The eyes should be full, but not protruding. The puppy can be of any color.

The puppy should be outgoing and friendly. If there is an opportunity, watch how the puppy interacts with other puppies and adult dogs. Chihuahuas overall are a healthy and sturdy breed. Their diminutive size, however, may be a drawback where there are small children and large dogs present. A Chihuahua may display a soft spot (fontanel) on the top of his head. This is known as the molera. While the molera may be open, it is not life-threatening nor does it predispose the Chihuahua to hydrocephalus.

Occasional brushing of the Smooth Coat variety to promote healthy skin and hair is recommended. More frequent brushing of the Long Coat variety should be planned. An occasional bath and periodic trimming of nails should be a part of a healthy grooming routine. As with all toy breeds, special attention to dental hygiene is a must. Providing hard bones and chew toys will help strengthen gums and remove tartar from teeth. Regular tooth brushing is essential to keeping the Chihuahua's teeth healthy. An occasional visit to the vet for a dental cleaning may be appropriate when these other outlets aren't enough.

The Chihuahua is highly intelligent. Obedience training should be considered to ensure he becomes a well-behaved companion.

COMPETITION

Chihuahuas compete in conformation classes as well as in Junior Showmanship for children and young adults. Chihuahuas successfully participate in agility, obedience, rally, and tracking events.

Official Standard for the Chihuahua

General Appearance: A graceful, alert, swift-moving compact little dog with saucy expression, and with terrier-like qualities of temperament.

Size, Proportion, Substance: *Weight*—A well balanced little dog not to exceed 6 pounds. *Proportion*—The body is off-square; hence, slightly longer when measured from point of shoulder to point of buttocks than height at the withers. Somewhat shorter bodies are preferred in males. *Disqualification*—Any dog over 6 pounds in weight.

Head: A well rounded "apple dome" skull, with or without molera. *Expression*—Saucy. *Eyes*—Full, round, but not protruding, balanced, set well apart—luminous dark or luminous ruby. Light eyes in blond or white-colored dogs permissible. Blue eyes or a difference in the color of the iris in the two eyes, or two different colors within one iris should be considered a serious fault. *Ears*—Large, erect type ears, held more upright when alert, but flaring to the sides at a 45-degree angle when in repose, giving breadth between the ears. *Stop*—Well defined. When viewed in profile, it forms a near 90-degree angle where muzzle joins skull. *Muzzle*—Moderately short, slightly pointed. Cheeks and jaws lean. *Nose*—Self-colored in blond types, or black. In moles, blues, and chocolates, they are self-colored. In blond types, pink noses permissible. *Bite*—Level or scissors. Overshot or undershot, or any distortion of the bite or jaw, should be penalized as a serious fault. A missing tooth or two is permissible. *Disqualifications*—Broken down or cropped ears.

Neck, Topline, Body: *Neck*—Slightly arched, gracefully sloping into lean shoulders. *Topline*—Level. *Body*—Ribs rounded and well sprung (but not too much "barrel-shaped"). *Tail*—Moderately long, carried sickle either up or out, or in a loop over the back with tip just touching the back. (Never tucked between legs.) *Disqualifications*— Docked tail, bobtail.

Forequarters: *Shoulders*—Lean, sloping into a slightly broadening support above straight forelegs that set well under, giving free movement at the elbows. Shoulders should be well up, giving balance and soundness, sloping into a level back (never down or low). This gives a well developed chest and strength of forequarters. *Feet*—A small, dainty foot with toes well split up but not spread, pads cushioned. (Neither the hare nor the cat foot.) Dewclaws may be removed. *Pasterns*—Strong.

Hindquarters: Muscular, with hocks well apart, neither out nor in, well let down, firm and sturdy. *Angulation*—Should equal that of forequarters. The feet are as in front. Dewclaws may be removed.

Coat: In the *Smooth Coats*, the coat should be of soft texture, close and glossy. (Heavier coats with undercoats permissible.) Coat placed well over body with ruff on neck preferred, and more scanty on head and ears. Hair on tail preferred furry. In *Long Coats*, the coat should be of a soft texture, either flat or slightly wavy, with undercoat preferred. *Ears*—Fringed. *Tail*—Full and long (as a plume). Feathering on feet and legs, pants on hind legs and large ruff on the neck desired and preferred. (The Chihuahua should be groomed only to create a neat appearance.) *Disqualification*—In Long Coats, too thin coat that resembles bareness.

Color: Any color—Solid, marked or splashed.

Gait: The Chihuahua should move swiftly with a firm, sturdy action, with good reach in front equal to the drive from the rear. From the rear, the hocks remain parallel to each other, and the foot fall of the rear legs follows directly behind that of the forelegs. The legs, both front and rear, will tend to converge slightly toward a central line of gravity as speed increases. The side view shows good, strong drive in the rear and plenty of reach in the front, with head carried high. The topline should remain firm and the backline level as the dog moves.

Temperament: Alert, projecting the "terrier-like" attitudes of self importance, confidence, self-reliance.

Disqualifications: Any dog over 6 pounds in weight. Broken down or cropped ears. Docked tail, bobtail. In Long Coats, too thin coat that resembles bareness.

Approved August 12, 2008
Effective October 1, 2008

Meet the Chinese Crested

Recognized by AKC® in 1991
American Chinese Crested Club, formed in 1979

Chinese Crested

Traits
- Affectionate
- Lively
- Devoted

60   AKC® Official Guide to Toy Dogs

HISTORY

Although the origin of the hairless dog has not been definitively established, it is believed that the Chinese Crested and other hairless dogs share a common ancestry. The Chinese Crested is an ancient breed, dating as far back as the 1500s. Allegedly, early Chinese explorers and traders took these dogs with them on their ships, and they frequently sold or traded the dogs with people they met along the way. Consequently, Cresteds have been found in port cities wherever Chinese ships have visited. Chinese Cresteds arrived in the United States in the 1800s, and a few devoted followers exhibited the breed in the early 1900s. Debra Woods established the preliminary registry of hairless dogs in the 1930s. The Chinese Crested was shown in the Miscellaneous Class from 1955 to 1965, when it was removed from eligibility due to low entries.

Before the Chinese Crested again achieved AKC® recognition, there were many devoted American supporters. Among these was famous actress and stripper Gypsy Rose Lee, who was a well-known Crested breeder for many years. Since their acceptance by AKC® in 1991, these enchanting little dogs have become a more common sight, often seen on TV and in movies.

FORM AND FUNCTION

Although hairlessness is the outstanding breed characteristic, Cresteds also come in a fully-coated variety called Powderpuff. Since the breed comes in any color from black to white and everything in-between (including blue, lavender, and pink—skin, that is) and in a size range of 11 to 13 inches, which is effectively everything from "tuck under your arm" to "walk along beside you," there is truly something to suit everyone! Chinese Cresteds not only serve as companions for many owners but also are true therapy dogs, whether trained or not, because they are great comforts to many people suffering from chronic conditions.

LIVING WITH A CRESTED

In Chinese Cresteds, hairlessness is relative. Some dogs are truly hairless, with only a few strands on their head, feet, and tail, while others are genetically hairless, yet sport a single haircoat over their entire bodies. Between these two extremes are many different hairless patterns. Show dogs may require some hair removal. Pets may be left au naturel. Often, the really hairy ones are trimmed as though they were Schnauzers or Poodles and look simply adorable. There is also a wide variation in size. Show dogs should be between 11 and 13 inches at the shoulder—pets may be larger or smaller.

If a hairless is your choice, cleanliness and protecting the skin from the sun are very important. The Powderpuff needs to be brushed daily to remain clean and pleasant to pet. The coat on a Powderpuff is different from most "hairy" breeds—the undercoat is shorter and the outer coat is a veil overlay. The result is a dog who is much easier to brush than most coated breeds.

Whatever the coat (or lack thereof), color, or size—a Crested wants nothing more than your love!

COMPETITION

Because of their strong love for their people, Chinese Cresteds are always eager to join in activities. In the world of AKC®, agility is a great adventure for many Cresteds, as is lure coursing, in which Cresteds are very enthusiastic and competitive. Obedience can be fun for both dog and handler, although gentle patience is necessary for this tenderhearted pet.

Official Standard for the Chinese Crested

General Appearance: A toy dog, fine-boned, elegant and graceful. The distinct varieties are born in the same litter. The Hairless with hair only on the head, tail and feet and the Powderpuff, completely covered with hair. The breed serves as a loving companion, playful and entertaining.

Size, Proportion, Substance: *Size*—Ideally 11 to 13 inches. However, dogs that are slightly larger or smaller may be given full consideration. *Proportion*—Rectangular—proportioned to allow for freedom of movement. Body length from withers to base of tail is slightly longer than the height at the withers. *Substance*—Fine-boned and slender but not so refined as to appear breakable or alternatively not a robust, heavy structure.

Head: *Expression*—Alert and intense. *Eyes*—Almond-shaped, set wide apart. Dark-colored dogs have dark-colored eyes, and lighter-colored dogs may have lighter-colored eyes. Eye rims match the coloring of the dog. *Ears*—Uncropped large and erect, placed so that the base of the ear is level with the outside corner of the eye. *Skull*—The skull is arched gently over the occiput from ear to ear. Distance from occiput to stop equal to distance from stop to tip of nose. The head is wedge-shaped viewed from above and the side. *Stop*—Slight but distinct. *Muzzle*—Cheeks taper cleanly into the muzzle. *Nose*—Dark in dark-colored dogs; may be lighter in lighter-colored dogs. Pigment is solid. *Lips*—Lips are clean and tight. *Bite*—Scissors or level in both varieties. Missing teeth in the Powderpuff are to be faulted. The Hairless variety is not to be penalized for absence of full dentition.

Neck, Topline, Body: *Neck*—Neck is lean and clean, slightly arched from the withers to the base of the skull and carried high. *Topline*—Level to slightly sloping croup. *Body*—Brisket extends to the elbow. Breastbone is not prominent. Ribs are well developed. The depth of the chest tapers to a moderate tuck-up at the flanks. Light in loin.

Tail—Tail is slender and tapers to a curve. It is long enough to reach the hock. When dog is in motion, the tail is carried gaily and may be carried slightly forward over the back. At rest the tail is down with a slight curve upward at the end resembling a sickle. In the Hairless variety, two-thirds of the end of the tail is covered by long, flowing feathering referred to as a plume. The Powderpuff variety's tail is completely covered with hair.

Forequarters: *Angulation*—Layback of shoulders is 45 degrees to point of shoulder allowing for good reach. *Shoulders*—Clean and narrow. *Elbows*—Close to body. *Legs*—Long, slender and straight. *Pasterns*—Upright, fine and strong. Dewclaws may be removed. *Feet*—Hare foot, narrow with elongated toes. Nails are trimmed to moderate length.

Hindquarters: *Angulation*—Stifle moderately angulated. From hock joint to ground perpendicular. Dewclaws may be removed. *Feet*—Same as forequarters.

Coat: The Hairless

socks). The texture of all hair is soft and silky, flowing to any length. Placement of hair is not as important as overall type. Areas that have hair usually taper off slightly. Wherever the body is hairless, the skin is soft and smooth. Head crest begins at the stop and tapers off between the base of the skull and the back of the neck. Hair on the ears and face is permitted on the Hairless and may be trimmed for neatness in both varieties. Tail plume is described under Tail. The Powderpuff variety is completely covered with a double soft and silky coat. Close examination reveals long thin guard hairs over the short silky undercoat. The coat is straight, of moderate density and length. Excessively heavy, kinky or curly coat is to be penalized. Grooming is minimal, consisting of presenting a clean and neat appearance.

Color: Any color or combination of colors.

Gait: Lively, agile and smooth without being stilted or hackneyed. Comes and goes at a trot moving in a straight line.

Temperament: Gay and alert.

Approved June 12, 1990
Effective April 1, 1991

Meet the English Toy Spaniel

Recognized by AKC® in 1886
English Toy Spaniel Club of America (englishtoyspanielclubofamerica.org), formed in 1903

Traits
- Happy
- Playful
- Willing to Please

HISTORY

During Tudor times (1485–1603), toy spaniels were common as ladies' pets. They were used as lap and foot warmers and even eliminated pesky fleas from their humans. But it was during the reign of the Stuarts (1603–1714) that these dogs were given the royal title of King Charles Spaniels.

King Charles II grew up loving small spaniels and was seldom seen without two or three dogs at his heels. So fond was the monarch of his little dogs, he wrote a decree that the King Charles Spaniel should be accepted in any public place, even in the Houses of Parliament, where animals were not usually allowed. This decree is still in existence in England today.

The little dogs were universally known as King Charles Spaniels, often referred to as Charlies. King Charles II's Charlies enjoyed full run of the palaces. Samuel Pepys, writing at the time, was critical of the king's devotion to them, noting that: "All I observed there was the silliness of the King playing with his dog all the while and not minding his business."

A medieval scoffer described the "Spaniell gentle… These dogs-pretty, proper and tine to satisfie the delicatenes of dainty dames and wanton women's wills …"

Indulged and pampered by the wealthy, King Charles Spaniels were known as "comforters." Of course, they were mostly admired just for their companionship, but they were also useful as foot warmers in cold and drafty English castles. A favorite legend tells that when Mary Queen of Scots was sent to her death in 1587, her executioner found one of her devoted little spaniels hidden in the folds of her skirt.

As court favors changed, so did the King Charles Spaniel, and crosses to toy dogs from Asia were likely. Soon the "comforters" became even smaller, with the extreme brachycephalic face, domed head, prominent eyes, and muzzle shortened so the nose was nearly flush to the face. They still had the charming spaniel personalities within a new contour. It is this short-faced version that has arrived at the present time as the English Toy Spaniel.

Black and tan appears to have been the King's favorite color, and early breeding programs emphasized this variety. Historians have noted that families of privilege had their favorites, and breeding programs closely aligned with development of a single variety and purpose. The Blenheim color was named after the family estate of the Dukes of Marlborough, whose family owned many of the red and whites over the years.

Although the breed in England goes by the name King Charles Spaniel, since 1886 the AKC® has recognized it as the English Toy Spaniel.

FORM AND FUNCTION

Ever since there were spaniels, toy versions have curled in laps and warmed hearts. In England and on the Continent, the charming spaniel personality in a tiny package was valued as a pet. These dogs were selected for smaller size among the existing dogs that established the type for the spaniels. Crosses to other tiny dogs may have occurred as well, but these were basically little gun dogs. Their most desirable weight is 8 to 14 pounds, but general symmetry and substance are more important than the actual weight. They should be compact and essentially square, built on cobby lines, and their coats should be long, wavy, silky, and profuse. Tails are docked and carried level with the back. Ears and their heavy feathering are so long as to nearly brush the ground.

LIVING WITH A CHARLIE

The Charlie is quiet and happy, content to be with his owners, forgiving in nature, and physically fastidious. Although an adornment to many owners desiring a merry, affectionate dog of distinction, the English Toy

Spaniel was said to be a fine small hunting spaniel, particularly on woodcock. Charlies are easygoing dogs and make excellent companions for city dwellers in small apartments who can provide the dogs regular walks on lead. These dogs do not like hot weather and should not be left outdoors on hot days. Twice-weekly brushing will keep their coats looking silky.

COMPETITION

English Toys can be stubborn during training, but they can be shown in conformation and all companion events. They also excel as therapy dogs.

Official Standard for the English Toy Spaniel

General Appearance: The English Toy Spaniel is a compact, cobby and essentially square toy dog possessed of a short-nosed, domed head, a merry and affectionate demeanor and a silky, flowing coat. His compact, sturdy body and charming temperament, together with his rounded head, lustrous dark eye, and well cushioned face, proclaim him a dog of distinction and character. The important characteristics of the breed are exemplified by the head.

Size, Proportion, Substance: *Size*—The most desirable weight of an adult is 8 to 14 pounds. General symmetry and substance are more important than the actual weight; however, all other things being equal, the smaller sized dog is to be preferred. *Proportion*—Compact and essentially square in shape, built on cobby lines. *Substance*—Sturdy of frame, solidly constructed.

Head: Head large in comparison to size, with a plush, chubby look, albeit with a degree of refinement which prevents it from being coarse. Expression—Soft and appealing, indicating an intelligent nature. Eyes—Large and very dark brown or black, set squarely on line with the nose, with little or no white showing. The eye rims should be black. Ears—Very long and set low and close to the head, fringed with heavy feathering. Skull—High and well domed; from the side, curves as far out over the eyes as possible. Stop—Deep and well-defined. Muzzle—Very short, with the nose well laid back and with well developed cushioning under the eyes. Jaw—Square, broad, and deep, and well turned up, with lips properly meeting to give a finished appearance. Nose—Large and jet black in color, with large, wide open nostrils. Bite—Slightly undershot; teeth not to show. A wry mouth should be penalized; a hanging tongue is extremely objectionable.

Neck, Topline, Body: *Neck*—Moderate in length; nicely arched. *Topline*—Level. *Body*—Short, compact, square and deep, on cobby lines, with a broad back. Sturdy of frame, with good rib and deep brisket.

Tail: The tail is docked to 2 to 4 inches in length and carried at or just slightly above the level of the back. The set of the tail is at the back's level. Many are born with a shorter or screw tail which is acceptable. The feather on the tail should be silky and from 3 to 4 inches in length, constituting a marked "flag" of a square shape. The tail and its carriage is an index of the breed's attitude and character.

Forequarters: Shoulders well laid back; legs well boned and strong, dropping straight down from the elbow; strong in pastern. Feet, front and rear, are neat and compact; fused toes are often seen and are acceptable.

Hindquarters: Rear legs are well muscled and nicely angulated to indicate strength, and parallel of hock.

Coat: Profusely coated, heavy fringing on the ears, body, and on the chest, and with flowing feathering on both the front and hind legs, and feathering on the feet. The coat is straight or only slightly wavy, with a silken, glossy texture. Although the Blenheim and the Ruby rarely gain the length of coat and ears of the Prince Charles and King Charles, good coats and long ear fringes are a desired and prized attribute. Over-trimming of the body, feet or tail fringings should be penalized.

Color: The *Blenheim* (red and white) consists of a pearly white ground with deep red or chestnut markings evenly distributed in large patches. The ears and the cheeks are red, with a blaze of white extending from the nose up the forehead and ending between the ears in a crescentic curve. It is preferable that there be red markings around both eyes. The Blenheim often carries a thumb mark or "Blenheim Spot" placed on the top and the center of the skull.

The *Prince Charles* (tricolor) consists of a pearly white ground, with evenly distributed black patches, solid black ears and black face markings. It is preferable that there be black markings around both eyes. The tan markings are of a rich color, and on the face, over the eyes, in the lining of the ears, and under the tail.

The **King Charles** (black and tan) is a rich, glossy black with bright mahogany tan markings appearing on the cheeks, lining of the ears, over the eyes, on the legs and underneath the tail. The presence of a small white chest patch about the size of a quarter or a few white hairs on the chest of a King Charles Spaniel are not to be penalized; other white markings are an extremely serious fault.

The **Ruby** is a self-colored, rich mahogany red. The presence of a small white chest patch about the size of a quarter or a few white hairs on the chest of a Ruby Spaniel are not to be penalized. Other white markings are an extremely serious fault.

Gait: Elegant with good reach in the front, and sound, driving rear action. The gait as a whole is free and lively, evidencing stable character and correct construction. In profile, the movement exhibits a good length of stride, and viewed from front and rear it is straight and true, resulting from straight-boned fronts and properly made and muscled hindquarters.

Temperament: The English Toy Spaniel is a bright and interested little dog, affectionate and willing to please.

Approved June 13, 1989
Effective August 1, 1989

Meet the Havanese

Recognized by AKC® in 1996
Havanese Club of America (havanese.org), formed in 1979

Traits
- Curious
- Observant
- Playful

HISTORY

The Havanese is the national dog of Cuba and the island nation's only existing native breed. Dogs of the bichon family were brought to Cuba and adapted to the island's diet and climate, resulting in a smaller dog than his predecessors, with a completely white silky-textured coat. That dog was the Blanquito de la Habana, also known as the Havana Silk Dog.

In the nineteenth century, Poodles arrived in Cuba from other countries. The result of crossbreeding Poodles to the Blanquito de la Habana was a slightly larger dog of various colors who retained the silky coat and bichon type. That dog is the Havanese.

At the start of the Cuban Revolution, many natives left their country. Some families brought Havanese with them to the United States, where they caught the eye of Mrs. Dorothy Goodale, an American dog breeder. She purchased eleven Havanese, and by 1974, a breeding program was underway in the United States. Goodale and other breeders founded the Havanese Club of America in 1979. Havanese have become a much-in-demand pet in recent years, and today they rank in the top quarter in breed registrations by the AKC®.

FORM AND FUNCTION

Havanese were developed to be ideal, small, beautiful house pets. Their compact, sturdy size; soft, silky coat of many colors; friendly, happy disposition; and their strong desire to be with their family all contribute to their roles as household pets and family entertainers.

LIVING WITH A HAVANESE

An attentive, loving owner who is at home most of the time is ideal for this charming dog. Havanese thrive on plenty of attention from family members. Gentle, patient training will result in a wonderful companion dog. Although busy and curious, Havanese are highly intelligent and trained easily. They are affectionate with people, dogs, and other pets. Havanese do well in both houses and apartments. They love to watch what's going on from up high, and you will often find them on the back of a sofa surveying their world.

Havanese get along with other nonaggressive pets. Although they are generally friendly with children, they are not a good choice for families with young children who are quick and active. Children need to be supervised around a small puppy to prevent injury to the puppy and the child.

Happiest when someone is at home with them, Havanese do not do well left alone for hours at a time. Running in a fenced yard is ideal, but regular leash walking and romping inside the home provide adequate exercise. The long coat requires regular brushing and combing to prevent matting. Pet coats may be trimmed to simplify coat maintenance.

House-training requires a regular routine and a dedicated owner, since they need to relieve themselves more frequently due to their small size. Until reliably trained, puppies should be confined to a small area and not given run of the house.

COMPETITION

Havanese participate in conformation classes at dog shows and in all companion events, including tracking. Since they are such athletic, intelligent little dogs, Havanese compete successfully with all other breeds, frequently winning top awards. Havanese also excel as therapy dogs.

Official Standard for the Havanese

General Appearance: The Havanese is a small, sturdy dog of immense charm. The native dog of Cuba, he is beloved as a friendly, intelligent and playful companion. He is slightly longer than tall, with a long, untrimmed, double coat. The Havanese has a short upper arm with moderate shoulder layback and a straight topline that rises slightly from the withers to the croup. The plumed tail is carried arched forward up over the back. The unique springy gait is a result of the breed's structure and playful, spirited personality. These characteristics of temperament, coat, structure and gait are essential to type.

Size, Proportion, Substance: The ideal height is between 9 and 10½ inches, with an acceptable height range from 8½ to 11½ inches. Height at withers under 8½ inches or over 11½ inches is a disqualification, except that the minimum height shall not apply to dogs or bitches under twelve months of age. The height is slightly less than the length from the point of shoulder to point of buttocks, creating a rectangular outline. The Havanese is moderately boned and should never appear coarse or fragile.

Head: The *expression* is soft, intelligent and mischievous. *Eyes* are large, dark brown and almond-shaped. Chocolate dogs may have somewhat lighter brown eyes. Eye rims are solid black for all colors except for chocolate dogs which have solid brown eye rims. Incomplete or total lack of pigmentation of the eye rims is a disqualification. *Ears* are broad at the base, dropped, and have a distinct fold. They are set high on the skull, slightly above the endpoint of the zygomatic arch. When alert, the ears lift at the base but always remain folded. Ear leather, when extended, reaches halfway to the nose. The *skull* is broad and slightly rounded. The stop is moderate and the planes of the head are level. The cheeks are flat. Length of *muzzle* is slightly less than length of skull measured from stop to point of occiput. The muzzle is full and rectangular with a broad nose. The nose and lips are solid black for all colors except for chocolate dogs which have solid brown pigment. Incomplete or total lack of pigmentation of the nose or lips is a disqualification. Any color pigmentation other than black or brown on the eye rims, nose or lips is a disqualification. Small depigmented areas on lips due to rubbing against canine teeth will not disqualify. A scissors *bite* is ideal and a full complement of incisors is preferred.

Neck, Topline, Body: The *neck* is slightly arched, of moderate length, blends smoothly into the shoulders and is in balance with the height and length of the dog. The prosternum is evident but not prominent. The chest is deep, well developed, and reaches the elbow. The straight *topline* rises slightly from the withers to the croup. Measured from point of shoulder to point of buttocks, the *body* is slightly longer than the height at the withers. This length comes from the ribcage. Ribs are well sprung. The loin is short and well muscled. There is a moderate tuck-up. The *tail* is high-set and arches forward up over the back. It is plumed with long, silky hair. The tail plume may fall straight forward or to either side of the body. While standing, a dropped tail is permissible. The tail may not be docked.

Forequarters: The tops of the shoulder blades lie in at the withers, allowing the neck to blend smoothly into the back. Moderate shoulder layback is sufficient to carry the head and neck high. The upper arm is short. Elbows are tight to the body and forelegs are straight when viewed from any angle. The length from the foot to the elbow is equal to the length from elbow to withers. Pasterns are short, strong and flexible, very slightly sloping. Dewclaws may be removed. The feet have arched

AKC Official Guide to Toy Dogs

toes and point straight ahead. Pads and nails may be any color.

Hindquarters: The hind legs are muscular with moderate angulation. Hocks are well let down; pasterns are parallel from hock to foot. The croup is slightly higher than the withers. Dewclaws may be removed. The feet have arched toes and point straight ahead. Pads and nails may be any color.

Coat: Silky to the touch, the coat is soft and light in texture in both outer and undercoat, although the outer coat carries slightly more weight. The coat is long, abundant and wavy. It stands off the body slightly, but flows with movement. An ideal coat will permit the natural lines of the dog to be seen. Puppy coat may be shorter and have a softer texture than adult coat. A single, flat, frizzy or curly coat should be faulted. A coarse, wiry coat is a disqualification. A short, smooth coat with or without furnishings is a disqualification. The coat may be corded. Corded coats will naturally separate into wavy sections in young dogs and will in time develop into cords. Adult corded dogs will be completely covered with a full coat of tassel-like cords.

Color: All colors and marking patterns are permissible and are of equal merit. The skin may be any color.

Gait: The Havanese gait is springy. The characteristic spring is the result of the short upper arm combined with the rear drive. Front legs reach forward freely matching the moderate extension in the rear. On the move, the pads may be visible coming or going. The head is carried high and the slight rise in the topline holds under movement.

Temperament: The Havanese is friendly, playful, alert and intelligent with a sweet, non-quarrelsome disposition. Aggression or shyness should be faulted.

Presentation: Havanese should be shown as naturally as is consistent with good grooming. They may be shown either brushed or corded. The coat should be clean and well conditioned. In mature dogs, the length of the coat may cause it to fall to either side down the back but it should not be deliberately parted. Head furnishings are long and untrimmed, and may fall forward over the eyes or to both sides of the head; they may also be held in two small braids secured with plain elastic bands. The braids start above the inside corner of each eye and extend at least to the outside corner, forming the appearance of eyebrows. No other hair accessories are permitted. Minimal trimming of the anal and genital area is permissible but should not be noticeable on presentation. Hair on the feet and between the pads should be neatly trimmed. No other trimming or sculpting of the coat is permitted and is to be so severely penalized as to preclude placement. Havanese should be presented at a natural speed on a loose lead to properly assess the characteristic springy gait.

Faults: The foregoing description is that of the ideal Havanese. Any deviation from the above described dog must be penalized to the extent of the deviation.

Disqualifications: Height at withers under 8½ or over 11½ inches except that the minimum height shall not apply to dogs or bitches under twelve months of age. Incomplete or total lack of pigmentation of the eye rims. Incomplete or total lack of pigmentation of the nose or lips. Any color pigmentation other than black or brown on the eye rims, nose or lips. A coarse, wiry coat. A short, smooth coat with or without furnishings.

Approved August 9, 2011
Effective September 28, 2011

Meet the Italian Greyhound

Recognized by AKC® in 1886
Italian Greyhound Club of America (italiangreyhound.org), formed in 1954

Traits
- Athletic
- Sensitive
- Loving

Italian Greyhound

HISTORY

The smallest of the sighthounds, the Italian Greyhound is believed to have originated over two thousand years ago in the Mediterranean countries, a belief based on depictions of miniature greyhound-type dogs in the early artwork of the region and on archaeological discovery of small greyhound skeletons.

By the Middle Ages, the breed was found throughout Southern Europe and, in the sixteenth century, became a favorite of Italian nobility, who greatly prized miniature dogs and named them Piccolo Levriero Italiano, or Italian Greyhound. Spreading throughout Europe, the Italian Greyhound arrived in England in the seventeenth century. One of the most decorative dogs, the IG has attracted many artists and was a favorite of many Renaissance masters. Among the painters who depicted the breed are Amerighi da Caravaggio, Hans Memling, Rogier van der Weyden, Gerard David, and Hiëronymus Bosch. As favorites of European royalty, IGs were beloved by such famous owners as Catherine the Great of Russia, Frederick the Great, Princess Anne of Denmark, and Queen Victoria.

First registered with the AKC® in 1886, a few IGs appeared in US dog shows that year. By the end of World War I, numbers and quality were strong enough in America to send stock over for a new start in England, where the breed had become almost extinct. The Italian Greyhound Club of America was founded in 1954, and 1963 marked the first year in which an IG was awarded an all-breed Best in Show.

FORM AND FUNCTION

Clearly possessing the physique of a running breed, IGs are true miniature sighthounds. Whether these handsome streamlined dogs were created to hunt small animals or just to be loving and decorative household pets is not definitely known, but most IGs decidedly have the instinct to run and chase after small creatures. They have the ability to shift quickly between their extremely affectionate nature with their humans and the urge to go after something that catches their eye. Many have the desire and ability to bring down a rabbit close to their own size, an activity they usually perform as a pack.

LIVING WITH AN IG

Early socialization is a must for this little dog to fully develop his personality and to keep the puppies from becoming fearful or shy. IGs are active and athletic, so the new owner should not be looking for a 24/7 couch potato. The best owner for this breed is someone with time and energy to devote to interacting with his or her dog, both in the home and away from it. IGs are bright and imaginative but, like most hounds, can be stubborn. A good owner will love them for their innate charm and charismatic nature, as well as for their foibles.

IGs are extremely loving, sometimes to the point of neediness, but they can be aloof with strangers. They need to be with someone who has the time to spend with them, lavishing them with attention. They need positive training, much attention, and, above all, love. Housetraining can be difficult but isn't impossible. Grooming is minimal but teeth need frequent brushing and annual veterinary dental treatments. Nails should be trimmed or filed regularly. Because the delicate nature of the IG's long slim legs make fractures a concern, new owners need to "IG-proof" their homes. A couple of daily walks will keep an IG happily exercised. The IG is good with children old enough to understand that they must respect the dog and treat him gently. Most IGs truly enjoy bonding with their humans as they take part in fun activities such as agility and lure coursing.

COMPETITION

IGs can participate in many different AKC® events, including conformation, obedience, rally, and agility, as well as tracking and lure coursing.

Italian Greyhound

Official Standard for the Italian Greyhound

Description: The Italian Greyhound is very similar to the Greyhound, but much smaller and more slender in all proportions and of ideal elegance and grace.

Head: Narrow and long, tapering to nose, with a slight suggestion of stop. **Skull**—Rather long, almost flat. **Muzzle**—Long and fine. **Nose**—Dark. It may be black or brown or in keeping with the color of the dog. A light or partly pigmented nose is a fault. **Teeth**—Scissors bite. A badly undershot or overshot mouth is a fault. **Eyes**—Dark, bright, intelligent, medium in size. Very light eyes are a fault. **Ears**—Small, fine in texture; thrown back and folded except when alerted, then carried folded at right angles to the head. Erect or button ears severely penalized.

Neck: Long, slender and gracefully arched.

Body: Of medium length, short coupled; high at withers, back curved and drooping at hindquarters, the highest point of curve at start of loin, creating a definite tuck-up at flanks. **Shoulders**—Long and sloping. **Chest**—Deep and narrow.

Forelegs: Long, straight, set well under shoulder; strong pasterns, fine bone.

Hindquarters: Long, well-muscled thigh; hind legs parallel when viewed from behind, hocks well let down, well-bent stifle.

Feet: Harefoot with well-arched toes. Removal of dewclaws optional.

Tail: Slender and tapering to a curved end, long enough to reach the hock; set low, carried low. Ring tail a serious fault, gay tail a fault.

Coat: Skin fine and supple, hair short, glossy like satin and soft to the touch.

Color: Any color and markings are acceptable except that a dog with brindle markings and a dog with the tan markings normally found on black-and-tan dogs of other breeds must be disqualified.

Action: High stepping and free, front and hind legs to move forward in a straight line.

Size: Height at withers, ideally 13 inches to 15 inches.

Disqualifications: A dog with brindle markings. A dog with the tan markings normally found on black-and-tan dogs of other breeds.

Approved December 14, 1976

Meet the Japanese Chin

Recognized by AKC® in 1888, originally registered as Japanese Spaniel until 1977 Japanese Chin Club of America (japanesechinclubofamerica.org/), formed in 1912

Traits
- Independent
- Demure
- Charming

AKC Official Guide to Toy Dogs

Japanese Chin

HISTORY

The origin of the Japanese Chin is clouded in the mysticism of Far Eastern ancient rites. Small dogs were known to have crisscrossed the Silk Road accompanying travelers as both commodities to trade and companions on the long journey. Some of these dogs became the pets of Buddhist monks, who nurtured and mated various types in their sheltered monasteries. Eventually, they were given as gifts to traveling dignitaries.

Chin quickly assumed their rightful position in the imperial palaces, where they were closely kept and guarded for the imperial family by eunuchs who were charged with looking after the little dogs' every need and desire. Mere peasants were not allowed to own them, as the small dogs became treasures more valuable than gold.

Navigating the globe by ship soon changed the way merchants traded their goods during the fifteenth century. Traders from the West arrived by sea using merchant ships. Seeking goodwill and favorable deals, they always brought gifts for members of the local nobility and government, such as a couple of dogs from their native lands—some dogs were large hunters, while others were lapdogs. Eventually, these little dogs were crossed with the existing pai dogs, short-legged, short-headed companion dogs whose roots rested with the caravans of the Silk Road, and other varieties emerged. Merchants from Portugal, Italy, Spain, Holland, England, and later the United States traveled the seas in search of trade and wealth, changing the lives of all involved, including the little dogs.

The name Japanese Chin is actually a misnomer, for the breed owes its basic origins not to Japan but to China. It has long been surmised that the Japanese Chin and Pekingese were once the same breed, with the Pekingese having been bred out to create the short, bowed-legged, long-backed, pear-shaped bodied breed of dog known today.

With the exception of a small Dutch trading post and limited contacts through China and Korea, Japan closed its doors in 1636 to the outside world in an effort to prevent foreigners from further influencing its people and culture. This self-imposed isolationist policy lasted for more than two centuries. It was not until Commodore Matthew C. Perry opened Japan in the mid-1850s that Westerners again stepped foot in the country on a regular trading basis. Perry's ships returned home laden with many imperial gifts, including three pairs of small dogs for himself, President Pierce, and Queen Victoria. Only Perry's pair is known to have survived the voyage; the other four never reached their destinations. Perry gave his pair of imperial dogs to his daughter, Caroline Perry Belmont, who was married to August Belmont, the father of a future AKC® president. In 1863, Britain's Queen Alexandra received her first Chin as a gift shortly after marrying into the royal family and drew worldwide attention to the breed.

Recognized by the AKC® in 1888, the Japanese Spaniel—as the breed was known in the United States until 1977—became a favorite among the American upper crust. The breed quickly gained status in the hearts and minds of people all over America, and it stands midway in the list of AKC® registered breeds.

FORM AND FUNCTION

The Chin is small, compact, and fine-boned, with a luxuriant coat and a well-plumed tail held over his back.

LIVING WITH A CHIN

This is a unique breed—loving but independent, eager but stubborn, snooty but demure. The Japanese Chin is a naturally clean dog who is easy to bathe and housetrain. Sometimes referred to as wash-and-wear, the coat seldom mats, and no special grooming or scissoring is required. Chin will wash each other's faces and clean their feet at night. They prefer to be on top of things much as a cat does—a plush pile of pillows on the bed is their idea of a perfect spot for sleeping. They like simple living and are good-natured, playful, and mischievous. They are perfect companions for anyone, from the well-behaved young child to the semi-active adult. They are good travelers, whether by car, boat, plane, or bike basket.

If the breed has a drawback, it is that the Chin is too smart. You cannot own a Japanese Chin, for the Japanese Chin owns you! You cannot train a Chin, for the Chin trains you! And, in the words of many longtime breeders, once you have lived with one, you will never want to be without one. And, one is never enough!

COMPETITION

Chin are eligible to compete in conformation and all companion events. They make exceptional therapy dogs.

(The history section for the Japanese Chin was written by Sari Brewster Tietjen.)

Official Standard for the Japanese Chin

General Appearance: The Japanese Chin is a small, well balanced, lively, aristocratic toy dog with a distinctive Oriental expression. It is light and stylish in action. The plumed tail is carried over the back, curving to either side. The coat is profuse, silky, soft and straight. The dog's outline presents a square appearance.

Size, Proportion, Substance: *Size*—Ideal size is 8 to 11 inches at the highest point of the withers. *Proportion*—Length between the sternum and the buttock is equal to the height at the withers. *Substance*—Solidly built, compact, yet refined. Carrying good weight in proportion to height and body build.

Head: Expression—Bright, inquisitive, alert, and intelligent. The distinctive Oriental expression is characterized by the large broad head, large wide-set eyes, short broad muzzle, ear feathering, and the evenly patterned facial markings. Eyes—Set wide apart, large, round, dark in color, and lustrous. A small amount of white showing in the inner corners of the eyes is a breed characteristic that gives the dog a look of astonishment. **Ears**—Hanging, small, V-shaped, wide apart, set slightly below the crown of the skull. When alert, the ears are carried forward and downward. The ears are well feathered and fit into the rounded contour of the head. **Skull**—Large, broad, slightly rounded between the ears but not domed. Forehead is prominent, rounding toward the nose. Wide across the level of the eyes. In profile, the forehead and muzzle touch on the same vertical plane of a right angle whose horizontal plane is the top of the skull. **Stop**—Deep. **Muzzle**—Short and broad with well-cushioned cheeks and rounded upper lips that cover the teeth. **Nose**—Very short with wide, open nostrils. Set on a level with the middle of the eyes and upturned. Nose leather is black in the black and white and the black and white with tan points, and is self-colored or black in the red and white. **Bite**—The jaw is wide and slightly undershot. A dog with one or two missing or slightly misaligned teeth should not be severely penalized. The Japanese Chin is very sensitive to oral examination. If the dog displays any hesitancy, judges are asked to defer to the handler for presentation of the bite.

Neck, Topline, Body: *Neck*—Moderate in length and thickness. Well set on the shoulders enabling the dog to carry its head up proudly. *Topline*—Level. *Body*—Square, moderately wide in the chest with rounded ribs. Depth of rib extends to the elbow. *Tail*—Set on high, carried arched up over the back and flowing to either side of the body.

Forequarters: Legs—Straight, and fine boned, with the elbows set close to the body. Removal of dewclaws is optional. Feet—Hare-shaped with feathering on the ends of the toes in the mature dog. Point straight ahead or very slightly outward.

Hindquarters: Legs—Straight as viewed from the rear and fine boned. Moderate bend of stifle. Removal of dewclaws is optional. Feet—Hare-shaped with feathering on the ends of the toes in the mature dog. Point straight ahead.

Coat: Abundant, straight, single, and silky. Has a resilient texture and a tendency to stand out from the body, especially on neck, shoulders, and chest areas where the hair forms a thick mane or ruff. The tail is profusely coated and forms a plume. The rump area is heavily coated and forms culottes or pants. The head and muzzle are covered with short hair except for the heavily feathered ears. The forelegs have short hair blending into profuse feathering on the backs of the legs. The rear legs have the previously described culottes, and in mature dogs, light feathering from hock joint to the foot.

Color: Either black and white, red and white, or black and white with tan points. The term tan points shall include tan or red spots over each eye, inside the ears, on both cheeks, and at the anal vent area if displaying any black. The term red shall include all shades of red, orange, and lemon, and sable, which includes any aforementioned shade intermingled or overlaid with black. Among the allowed colors there shall be no preference when judging. A clearly defined white muzzle and blaze are preferable to a solidly marked head. Symmetry of facial markings is preferable. The size, shape, placement or number of body patches is not of great importance. The white is clear of excessive ticking. Disqualification—Any color not listed.

Gait: Stylish and lively in movement. Moves straight with front and rear legs following in the same plane.

Temperament: A sensitive and intelligent dog whose only purpose is to serve man as a companion. Responsive and affectionate with those it knows and loves but reserved with strangers or in new situations.

Disqualifications: Any color not listed.

Approved October 11, 2011
Effective November 30, 2011

Meet the Maltese

Recognized by AKC® in 1888
American Maltese Association (americanmaltese.org), formed in 1961

Traits
- Bright
- Playful
- Gentle

HISTORY

That the Maltese is a very old breed is of no doubt. It has been known by a variety of names: Melitaie Dog, Ye Ancient Dogge of Malta, Roman Ladies Dog, the Comforter, the Spaniel Gentle, Bichon, Shock Dog, Maltese Lion Dog, and Maltese Terrier. It is now simply the Maltese.

Historians agree that the breed is native to the Mediterranean area, either the island of Malta, or Melita. Because Maltese were so prized, they were often sold and traded, thus making their way around the world. The Greeks and Romans seemed particularly enthralled by the Maltese because there are many stories, paintings, and ceramic art depicting the breed.

By the Middles Ages, Maltese were being imported through trade to European royalty. They were primarily sought for the pleasure and amusement of women. The emphasis of smallness was important, so that the women could carry them in their bosoms, sleeves, or arms. Descriptions varied from "the size of squirrels" to "not bigger than the common ferret."

Maltese were among some of the early breeds to be exhibited at English dog shows starting in the 1860s. The Maltese was accepted in the AKC® Stud Book in 1888, but were rare in the United States until around the 1950s. Some of the breed's well-known admirers include Queen Elizabeth I, Queen Victoria, Liberace, Gary Cooper, John Davidson, Totie Fields, Britney Spears, and, of course, Elizabeth Taylor.

FORM AND FUNCTION

The original and, to this day, sole purpose of the Maltese is to be a companion. This small toy dog weighs between 4 and 6 pounds and is covered with a mantle of white silky straight hair, setting off his dark eyes and black nose. Structural soundness is important in Maltese because, even though they are content to snuggle on a lap, they are most definitely not wallflowers. They do love to play, run, jump, and go for walks. Since Maltese have hair and don't shed, it is possible that a person who is allergic to dogs may be able to live with a Maltese. However, there is no such thing as a true hypoallergenic dog, so if anyone in the family has allergies, it is best to see whether a Maltese can be tolerated before adding one to a home.

LIVING WITH A MALTESE

Their size makes the Maltese great pets for people living in small spaces, such as city apartments. Easily portable, they don't require a great deal of exercise, but some activity such as a walk, a romp in the backyard, and playing fetch should be done on a daily basis to keep the dog fit. Male or female? With Maltese there is really no difference. The boys are just as affectionate and clean (if neutered before sexual maturity) as the girls.

It is not recommended that a Maltese puppy go to a home where there are young children. While Maltese do like children, they are tiny as puppies and the possibility of being stepped on or dropped by a child is an all too real scenario.

Be wary of the so-called "teacup" or "micromini" Maltese who can be found for sale on the Internet. These are Maltese that supposedly will end up at less than 3 pounds as adults. Maltese are not meant to be this tiny and as a result will often have health problems.

Maltese are highly intelligent and know very well how to use their charm to get their way. If given the chance, they can become easily spoiled. This isn't a problem for dog savvy owners, but many pet owners will give in, often resulting in a pet with poor manners.

The Maltese coat is its crowning glory. Whether kept in long hair or a cute puppy cut, brushing on a regular basis (often daily) is a must to keep the hair from tangling. In addition to home brushing, a regular visit to a pet groomer is part of owning a Maltese. The hair grows continuously, so trimming/clipping of the coat needs to be done. In short, if you are not prepared to deal with the coat, the Maltese is not for you.

It is not unusual for Maltese puppies to retain baby teeth after the adult teeth have come in. These baby teeth will need to be pulled if they do not fall out on their own. Also, Maltese are prone to developing tartar buildup and gingivitis, which could lead to early tooth loss.

COMPETITION

These bright, happy little dogs may compete and title in conformation and all companion events, and many work as therapy dogs. They are particularly adorable on an agility course.

Official Standard for the Maltese

General Appearance: The Maltese is a toy dog covered from head to foot with a mantle of long, silky, white hair. He is gentle-mannered and affectionate, eager and sprightly in action, and, despite his size, possessed of the vigor needed for the satisfactory companion.

Head: Of medium length and in proportion to the size of the dog. The *skull* is slightly rounded on top, the stop moderate. The *drop ears* are rather low set and heavily feathered with long hair that hangs close to the head. *Eyes* are set not too far apart; they are very dark and round, their black rims enhancing the gentle yet alert expression. The *muzzle* is of medium length, fine and tapered but not snipy. The *nose* is black. The *teeth* meet in an even, edge-to-edge bite, or in a scissors bite.

Neck: Sufficient length of neck is desirable as promoting a high carriage of the head.

Body: Compact, the height from the withers to the ground equaling the length from the withers to the root of the tail. Shoulder blades are sloping, the elbows well knit and held close to the body. The back is level in topline, the ribs well sprung. The chest is fairly deep, the loins taut, strong, and just slightly tucked up underneath.

Tail: A long-haired plume carried gracefully over the back, its tip lying to the side over the quarter.

Legs and Feet: Legs are fine-boned and nicely feathered. Forelegs are straight, their pastern joints well knit and devoid of appreciable bend. Hind legs are strong and moderately angulated at stifles and hocks. The feet are small and round, with toe pads black. Scraggly hairs on the feet may be trimmed to give a neater appearance.

Coat and Color: The coat is single, that is, without undercoat. It hangs long, flat, and silky over the sides of the body almost, if not quite, to the ground. The long head-hair may be tied up in a topknot or it may be left hanging. Any suggestion of kinkiness, curliness, or woolly texture is objectionable. Color, pure white. Light tan or lemon on the ears is permissible, but not desirable.

Size: Weight under 7 pounds, with from 4 to 6 pounds preferred. Overall quality is to be favored over size.

Gait: The Maltese moves with a jaunty, smooth, flowing gait. Viewed from the side, he gives an impression of rapid movement, size considered. In the stride, the forelegs reach straight and free from the shoulders, with elbows close. Hind legs to move in a straight line. Cowhocks or any suggestion of hind leg toeing in or out are faults.

Temperament: For all his diminutive size, the Maltese seems to be without fear. His trust and affectionate responsiveness are very appealing. He is among the gentlest mannered of all little dogs, yet he is lively and playful as well as vigorous.

Approved March 10, 1964

Meet the Manchester Terrier (Toy)

Recognized by AKC® in 1886
American Manchester Terrier Club (americanmanchester.org), formed in 1958

Traits
- Observant
- Devoted
- Spirited

HISTORY

The origins of the Toy Manchester Terrier can be traced to the Old English Black and Tan Terrier, which first appeared in print in the early 1800s, in a famous book by Stonehenge (John Henry Walsh) called The Dog in Health and Disease. Walsh describes the dog as possessing smooth hair, a long tapering nose, a narrow flat skull, small and bright eyes, a chest rather deep than wide, and black and tan as the only true color. This description serves today's standard of perfection quite well.

Gypsy was the first breed representative registered with the AKC® in 1887. In 1923, the Manchester Terrier Club of America was recognized. The breed name changed from English Toy (Black and Tan) Terrier to Toy Manchester Terrier in 1934, and four years later the American Toy Manchester Terrier Club was organized.

Toy Manchester Terriers became the "it" dogs in the 1940s, while the Standards' numbers dwindled. By the following decade, the Manchester Terrier Club of America was in need of representation, and the American Toy Manchester Terrier Club agreed to combine the two breeds into one with two varieties. In 1959, the AKC® recognized the Manchester Terriers as two varieties, Standard and Toy, and a new national breed club, the American Manchester Terrier Club, was formed.

FORM AND FUNCTION

Strong and agile, Manchester Terriers require compact, muscular bodies to do their bred-for jobs of dispatching vermin. Toy Manchester Terriers today have evolved into smaller versions of the Standards, thanks to the use of larger dogs in breeding programs. The only differences between the Toy and Standard varieties, according to the breed standard, concern size and ears. Toys are 12 pounds and under, while Standards weigh over 12 pounds, up to 22 pounds. The ears of the Toy Manchester are naturally erect only, although the Standard can have ears that are naturally erect, cropped, or button.

LIVING WITH A TOY MANCHESTER TERRIER

The Toy Manchester Terrier is an ideal companion for urban or suburban living. Select a puppy from a litter that's preferably recently awakened from a nap. Manchester pups are lively, zippy, curious tykes who love to explore people (their clothing and shoes) and everything around them. Healthy, sound pups should feel smooth and firm to the touch when picked up, if a little squirmy. The coat is composed of short, fine hair with no bald spots. Energetic and fun-loving, Manchesters are superb companions for older children and owners who enjoy being on the go.

A new owner should plan on activities that the two of you can share on a daily basis: explorative walks, playing ball, or learning cute tricks, to list just a few. Housetraining requires diligence, patience, and terrier tenacity on your part to be successful. Manchesters like to be warm, so their beds should be cozy, preferably with an extra blanket to snuggle under. Bathing is a snap, and shedding is minimal. Toy Manchesters are blessed with long lives and usually live to their upper teens.

COMPETITION

Toy Manchesters participate in conformation, tracking, lure coursing, earthdog, obedience, and agility, and in all companion events.

Official Standard for the Manchester Terrier

General Appearance: A small black short coated dog with distinctive rich mahogany markings and a taper style tail. In structure, the Manchester presents a sleek, sturdy yet elegant look and has a wedge shaped long and clean head with a keen, bright, alert expression. The smooth, compact, muscular body expresses great power and agility enabling the Manchester to kill vermin and course small game. Except for size and ear options, there are no differences between the Standard and Toy varieties of the Manchester Terrier. The Toy variety is a diminutive version of the Standard variety.

Size, Proportion, Substance: The Toy variety shall not exceed 12 pounds. It is suggested that clubs consider dividing the American-bred and Open classes by weight as follows: 7 pounds and under, over 7 pounds and not exceeding 12 pounds.

The Standard variety shall be over 12 pounds and not exceeding 22 pounds. Dogs weighing over 22 pounds shall be disqualified. It is suggested that clubs consider dividing the American-bred and Open classes by weight as follows: Over 12 pounds and not exceeding 16 pounds, over 16 pounds and not exceeding 22 pounds.

The Manchester Terrier, overall, is slightly longer than tall. The height, measured vertically from the ground to the highest point of the withers, is slightly less than the length, measured horizontally from the point of the shoulders to the rear projection of the upper thigh. The bone and muscle of the Manchester Terrier is of sufficient mass to ensure agility and endurance.

The Toy variety over 12 pounds shall be excused. Disqualification: Standard Variety—Weight over 22 pounds.

Head: The Manchester Terrier has a keen and alert *expression*. The nearly black, almond shaped *eyes* are small, bright and sparkling. They are set moderately close together slanting upwards on the outside. The eyes neither protrude nor sink in the skull. Eye lid and rim pigmentation is black.

Correct *ears* for the Standard variety are the naturally erect ear, the cropped ear or the button ear. No preference is given to any of the ear types. The naturally erect ear and button ear are wider at the base tapering to pointed tips and carried well up on the skull. Cropped ears are long, pointed and carried erect. The only correct ear for the Toy variety is the naturally erect ear. They are wider at the base tapering to pointed tips and carried well upon the skull. The *head* is long, narrow, tight skinned and almost flat with a slight indentation up the forehead. It resembles a blunted wedge in frontal and profile views. The *muzzle* and *skull* are equal in length. There is a visual effect of a slight stop as viewed in profile. The muzzle is well filled under the eyes with no visible cheek muscles. The underjaw is full and well defined and the nose is black. Tight black lips lie close to the jaw. The *bite* is a true scissors bite. Level bite is acceptable. The jaws are powerful with full and proper dentition. The teeth are white and strongly developed. Wide, flaring, blunt tipped, or "bell" ears are a serious fault for both varieties. Disqualification: Toy Variety—Cropped or button ears.

Neck, Topline, Body: The slightly arched *neck* is slim, graceful and of moderate length. It gradually becomes larger as it approaches and blends smoothly with the sloping shoulders. The *topline* shows a slight subtle arch over the robust loins falling slightly to the tail set. While standing or in motion, a flat or roached back is a serious fault for both varieties. The chest is narrow between the legs and deep in the brisket. The forechest is moderately defined. The ribs are well sprung, flattened in the lower end to permit clearance of the forelegs. The underline is tucked up extending in an arched line from the deep brisket. The taper style *tail* is moderately short reaching no further than the hock joint. It is set on at the end of the croup being thicker where it joins the body. The tail tapers to a point carried no higher than the back. While standing or in motion, a flat or roached back is a serious fault for both varieties.

Forequarters: The shoulder blades and the upper arm are relatively the same length. The distance from the elbow to the withers is approximately the same as the distance from the elbow to the ground. The elbows lie close to the brisket. The shoulders are well laid back. The forelegs are straight of proportionate length and placed well under the brisket. The pasterns are almost perpendicular. Dew claws may be removed. The front feet are compact and well arched. The two middle toes are slightly longer than the others. The pads are thick and toenails are jet black.

Hindquarters: The thigh is muscular with the length of the upper and lower thighs being approximately equal. The stifle is well turned. The hindquarters are in balance with the well laid back shoulders. The hocks are well let down. Dew claws may be removed. The hind feet are shaped like those of a cat with thick pads and jet-black nails.

Coat: The coat is smooth, short, dense, tight and glossy.

Color: The coat is jet black with rich mahogany tan which does not blend into each other, but abruptly form clear, well defined lines of color. There is a very small tan spot over each eye and a very small tan spot on each cheek. On the head, the muzzle is tanned to the nose. The nose and nasal bone are jet black. The tan extends under the throat ending in the shape of the letter V. The inside of the ears are partly tan. There are tan spots, called "rosettes" on each side of the chest above the front legs. These are more pronounced in puppies than in adults. There is a black "thumb mark" patch on the front of each foreleg at the pastern. The remainder of the foreleg is tan to the carpus joint. There is a distinct black "pencil mark" line running lengthwise on the top of each toe on all four feet. Tan on the hind leg should continue from the penciling on the toes up the inside of the legs to a little below the stifle joint. The outside of the hind legs is black. There is tan under the tail and on the vent but only of such size as to be covered by the tail. White on any part of the coat is a serious fault and a disqualification whenever the white forms a patch or stripe measuring as much as one half inch at its longest dimension. Any color other than black and tan shall be disqualified. Soundness and type supersede color and markings.

Gait: The gait is free and effortless with good reach of the forequarters. Rear quarters have strong, driving power to match the front reach. Hocks fully extend. Each rear leg moves in line with the foreleg of the same side, neither thrown in nor out. When moving at a trot, the legs converge toward the center of gravity of the dog.

Temperament: The Manchester Terrier is neither aggressive nor shy. He is keenly observant, devoted yet discerning. Not being a sparring breed, the Manchester Terrier is generally friendly with other dogs. Excessive shyness or aggressiveness shall be considered a serious fault.

Faults:
Toy Variety: Over 12 pounds shall be excused.
Both varieties:
Wide, flaring, blunt tipped or "bell" ears.
Flat or roached back while standing or in motion.
Excessive shyness or aggressiveness.
White on any part of the coat.

Disqualifications:
Standard Variety—Weight over 22 pounds. Toy Variety—Cropped or button ears.
Both Varieties—White on any part of the coat whenever the white forms a patch or stripe measuring as much as one half inch at its longest dimension.
Any color other than black and tan.

Approved July 13, 2021
Effective October 6, 2021

Meet the Miniature Pinscher

Recognized by AKC® in 1925
Miniature Pinscher Club of America (minpin.org), formed in 1930

Traits
- Fun-Loving
- Proud
- Fearless

Miniature Pinscher

HISTORY

The Miniature Pinscher originated in Germany. The first representation of the breed appears in a seventeenth-century painting of a cat-sized dog resembling the Miniature Pinscher of today. That makes the Miniature Pinscher an older breed than the Doberman Pinscher, which didn't emerge until the late 1800s.

Historians tell us that the Miniature Pinscher breed sprang from genetic crosses of the German Pinscher, the Dachshund, and the Italian Greyhound. From these ancestors, the Min Pin (as fanciers lovingly call him) gets his feistiness, fearlessness, speed, and grace. By the nineteenth century, the Reh Pinscher, as he was called in Germany, was essentially formed. The feisty and quick little dogs were used as vermin hunters (rats, mice, moles, and such creatures). Their size and speed enabled them to get close to the domestic pests and keep them from eating foodstuffs and wreaking havoc.

The Miniature Pinscher has had a fascinating history since its creation. Kept a secret in Germany and Scandinavia, the Min Pin was first imported into the United States around 1919. The AKC® registered the first Min Pin in 1925 under the breed name Pinscher (toy). The Miniature Pinscher Club of America started in 1930, when the breed was shown in the Terrier Group. The next year saw its reclassification as a toy breed called Pinscher (Miniature). It wasn't until 1972 that the breed was officially renamed the Miniature Pinscher.

Although the Min Pin has undergone many changes for the better over the years, especially as to shape of head, eyes, and general conformation, his character and love of his people remain unchanged. He is the ideal playmate and companion for young and old alike—all that one could wish for in a housedog—and admired and respected wherever he goes.

FORM AND FUNCTION

The Miniature Pinscher is structurally a well-balanced, sturdy, compact, short-coupled dog. He naturally is well groomed, proud, vigorous, and alert.

Characteristic traits are his hackney-like movement, fearless animation, complete self-possession, and his spirited presence. The Miniature Pinscher's size and shape allow him to be comfortable in many different environments. He is equally comfortable in a condominium, apartment, or country home.

LIVING WITH A MIN PIN

The Min Pin is a proud and fearless big dog in a little package. He is referred to as the "King of Toys" because he is spirited and brave and stands on his own. His self-confidence shines through, whether he is in his home, on a busy street, or at a local shopping center.

Min Pins are always on the alert as watchdogs, and owners say their pointy ears can hear a leaf drop. They are aloof toward strangers, but once they accept their owners' friends, they remember that relationship and are ready for attention from new friends.

They are adaptable enough to create their own exercise programs, yet can keep up with their owners on hikes. Min Pins are great with children who are taught how to handle small dogs and understand they are living, breathing animals not toys to be mishandled. Min Pins enjoy playing chase and tug-of-war but also need to know they can go away to a safe place to rest.

A Miniature Pinscher should be kept inside the home and in a fenced area when outdoors. They cannot tolerate cold temperatures and should be kept warm and dry in the winter. They prefer to be with their humans and are great for snuggling on a cold night or sitting on the porch swing in the summer.

The Miniature Pinscher is easy to care for, only requiring a good coat- and tooth brushing, an occasional bath, and nail clipping. Your breeder will be able to guide you, along with your veterinarian, about any health issues that arise. When training and living with a Min Pin, owners must have a sense of humor and lots of patience and be as adaptable as their dog.

COMPETITION

The Miniature Pinscher is a versatile dog, amazingly quick to learn agility, obedience, and even hunting. Since the breed was originally bred for exterminating vermin from the household, Min Pins are quick to defend their homes from snakes, rats, and mice. Miniature Pinschers are smart and learn quickly, thus being well suited to agility and obedience trials, as well as to the conformation ring.

Official Standard for the Miniature Pinscher

General Appearance: The Miniature Pinscher is structurally a well balanced, sturdy, compact, short-coupled, smooth-coated dog. He naturally is well groomed, proud, vigorous and alert. Characteristic traits are his hackney-like action, fearless animation, complete self-possession, and his spirited presence.

Size, Proportion, Substance: *Size*—10 to 12½ inches in height allowed, with desired height 11 to 11½ inches measured at highest point of the shoulder blades. Disqualification—Under 10 inches or over 12½ inches in height. Length of males equals height at withers. Females may be slightly longer.

Head: In correct proportion to the body. Tapering, narrow with well fitted but not too prominent foreface which balances with the skull. No indication of coarseness. Eyes full, slightly oval, clear, bright and dark even to a true black, including eye rims, with the exception of chocolates, whose eye rims should be self-colored. Ears set high, standing erect from base to tip. May be cropped or uncropped. Skull appears flat, tapering forward toward the muzzle. Muzzle strong rather than fine and delicate, and in proportion to the head as a whole. Head well balanced with only a slight drop to the muzzle, which is parallel to the top of the skull. Nose black only, with the exception of chocolates which should have a self-colored nose. Lips and cheeks small, taut and closely adherent to each other. Teeth meet in a scissors bite.

Neck, Topline, Body: *Neck* proportioned to head and body, slightly arched, gracefully curved, blending into shoulders, muscular and free from suggestion of dewlap or throatiness. *Topline*—Back level or slightly sloping toward the rear both when standing and gaiting. *Body* compact, slightly wedge-shaped, muscular. Forechest well developed. Well-sprung ribs. Depth of brisket, the base line of which is level with points of the elbows. Belly moderately tucked up to denote grace of structural form. Short and strong in loin. Croup level with topline. Tail set high, held erect, docked in proportion to size of dog.

Forequarters: Shoulders clean and sloping with moderate angulation coordinated to permit the hackney-like action. Elbows close to the body. Legs—Strong bone development and small clean joints. As viewed from the front, straight and upstanding. Pasterns strong, perpendicular.

Dewclaws should be removed. Feet small, catlike, toes strong, well arched and closely knit with deep pads. Nails thick, blunt.

Hindquarters: Well muscled quarters set wide enough apart to fit into a properly balanced body. As viewed from the rear, the legs are straight and parallel. From the side, well angulated. Thighs well muscled. Stifles well defined. Hocks short, set well apart. Dewclaws should be removed. Feet small, catlike, toes strong, well arched and closely knit with deep pads. Nails thick, blunt.

Coat: Smooth, hard and short, straight and lustrous, closely adhering to and uniformly covering the body.

Color: Solid clear red. Stag red (red with intermingling of black hairs). Black with sharply defined rust-red markings on cheeks, lips, lower jaw, throat, twin spots above eyes and chest, lower half of forelegs, inside of hind legs and vent region, lower portion of hocks and feet. Black pencil stripes on toes. Chocolate with rust-red markings the same as specified for blacks, except brown pencil stripes on toes. In the solid red and stag red a rich vibrant medium to dark shade is preferred. Disqualifications—Any color other than listed. Thumb mark (patch of black hair surrounded by rust on the front of the foreleg between the foot and the wrist; on chocolates, the patch is chocolate hair). White on any part of dog which exceeds ½ inch in its longest dimension.

Gait: The forelegs and hind legs move parallel, with feet turning neither in nor out. The hackney-like action is a high-stepping, reaching, free and easy gait in which the front leg moves straight forward and in front of the body and the foot bends at the wrist. The dog drives smoothly and strongly from the rear. The head and tail are carried high.

Temperament: Fearless animation, complete self-possession, and spirited presence.

Disqualifications: Under 10 inches or over 12½ inches in height. Any color other than listed. Thumb mark (patch of black hair surrounded by rust on the front of the foreleg between the foot and the wrist; on chocolates, the patch is chocolate hair). White on any part of dog which exceeds ½ inch in its longest dimension.

Approved July 8, 1980
Reformatted February 21, 1990

Meet the Papillon

Recognized by AKC® in 1915
Papillon Club of America (papillonclub.org), formed in 1935

Traits
- Outgoing
- Friendly
- Alert

HISTORY

Papillon means "butterfly" in French, although several countries lay claim to being the birthplace of these delicate toy dogs with the unique winglike ears. Dogs resembling the modern-day Papillon, once known as the Continental Toy Spaniel, grace the canvases of the old masters of Western Europe, including Rubens and Titian. Marie Antoinette is said to have given the breed its name, calling hers Petite Papillon, or "Little Butterfly."

Papillons alighted in the United States around 1907, and by 1915, they had gained AKC® recognition. While their primary occupation in Europe was to adorn royal laps, in America their brains, energy, and athleticism have attracted a loyal following.

FORM AND FUNCTION

A Papillon is a big dog in a little package and is the "do it all" toy dog. The hallmark of the breed is its big, beautiful butterfly ears. The ears are large and round and should be well fringed. The drop-eared Papillon is called a Phalene ("moth" in French) and was the original variety of the breed. The Papillon coat is silky and must be white with patches of color. Papillons are small, measuring between 8 and 11 inches at the withers and usually weighing 5 to 8 pounds.

LIVING WITH A PAPILLON

Papillons are companion animals who love to play and just be dogs. Given a choice, a Papillon would much rather be running around the house chasing a ball than sitting quietly. Not hyper dogs, Papillons are outgoing, with a fun-loving personality. They are very intelligent and easily trained, and, of course, it helps that they like to please and be with those they love! The temperament of a Papillon should be happy, alert, and friendly. Papillons have a zest for life and want to share that with their owners. They are perpetual puppies and very adaptable dogs, which makes adopting an adult a good option.

Papillons are not the right dogs for everyone, but for the right owners they make wonderful companions who will add joy to a home for many, many years. The breed is generally healthy and long-lived.

Breeders are careful with placement of Papillons in homes with large dogs, as Papillons can never be convinced that they are toy dogs. Breeders also strongly assess the placement of a Papillon in a home with small children. Since Papillons are fine-boned dogs, owners must be keenly aware that certain play or activity could lead to an injury.

Grooming a Papillon is a relatively easy task that requires only regular baths, nail clipping, and brushing. Dental care is very important for Papillons, as it is for all dogs but especially for toy dogs.

COMPETITION

With the rising interest in performance and companion events throughout the dog world, Papillons have become top-ranked toy dogs in obedience, agility, and tracking. They fly through agility courses and are ideal as therapy and service dogs.

Official Standard for the Papillon

General Appearance: The Papillon is a small, friendly, elegant toy dog of fine-boned structure, light, dainty and of lively action; distinguished from other breeds by its beautiful butterfly-like ears.

Size, Proportion, Substance: *Size*—Height at withers, 8 to 11 inches. Fault—Over 11 inches. Disqualification—Over 12 inches. *Proportion*—Body must be slightly longer than the height at withers. It is not a cobby dog. Weight is in proportion to height. *Substance*—Of fine-boned structure.

Head: *Eyes* dark, round, not bulging, of medium size and alert in expression. The inner corners of the eyes are on line with the stop. Eye rims black. *Ears*—The ears of either the erect or drop type should be large with rounded tips, and set on the sides and toward the back of the head. (1) Ears of the erect type are carried obliquely and move like the spread wings of a butterfly. When alert, each ear forms an angle of approximately 45 degrees to the head. The leather should be of sufficient strength to maintain the erect position. (2) Ears of the drop type, known as the Phalene, are similar to the erect type, but are carried drooping and must be completely down. Faults—Ears small, pointed, set too high; one ear up, or ears partly down. *Skull*—The head is small. The skull is of medium width and slightly rounded between the ears. A well-defined stop is formed where the muzzle joins the skull. *Muzzle*—The muzzle is fine, abruptly thinner than the head, tapering to the nose. The length of the muzzle from the tip of the nose to stop is approximately one-third the length of the head from tip of nose to occiput. *Nose* black, small, rounded and slightly flat on top. The following fault shall be severely penalized—Nose not black. *Lips* tight, thin and black. Tongue must not be visible when jaws are closed. *Bite*—Teeth must meet in a scissors bite. Faults—Overshot or undershot.

Neck, Topline, Body: *Neck* of medium length. *Topline*—The backline is straight and level. *Body*—The chest is of medium depth with ribs well sprung. The belly is tucked up. *Tail* long, set high and carried well arched over the body. The tail is covered with a long, flowing plume. The plume may hang to either side of the body. Faults—Low-set tail; one not arched over the back, or too short.

Forequarters: Shoulders well developed and laid back to allow freedom of movement. Forelegs slender, fine-boned and must be straight. Removal of dewclaws on forelegs optional. Front feet thin and elongated (hare-like), pointing neither in nor out.

Hindquarters: Well developed and well angulated. The hind legs are slender, fine-boned, and parallel when viewed from behind. Hocks inclined neither in nor out. Dewclaws, if any, must be removed from hind legs. Hind feet thin and elongated (hare-like), pointing neither in nor out.

Coat: Abundant, long, fine, silky, flowing, straight with resilient quality, flat on back and sides of body. A profuse frill on chest. There is no undercoat. Hair short and close on skull, muzzle, front of forelegs, and from hind feet to hocks. Ears well fringed, with the inside covered with silken hair of medium length. Backs of the forelegs are covered with feathers diminishing to the pasterns. Hind legs are covered to the hocks with abundant breeches (culottes). Tail is covered with a long, flowing plume. Hair on feet is short, but fine tufts may appear over toes and grow beyond them, forming a point.

Color: Always parti-color or white with patches of any color(s). On the head, color(s) other than white must cover both ears, back and front, and extend without interruption from the ears over both eyes. A clearly defined white blaze and noseband are preferred to a solidly marked head. Symmetry of facial markings is desirable. The size, shape, placement, and presence or absence of patches of color on the body are without importance. Among the colors there is no preference, provided nose, eye rims and lips are well pigmented black.

The following faults shall be severely penalized—Color other than white not covering both ears, back and front, or not extending from the ears over both eyes. A slight extension of the white collar onto the base of the ears, or a few white hairs interspersed among the color, shall not be penalized, provided the butterfly appearance is not sacrificed.

Disqualifications—An all-white dog or a dog with no white.

Gait: Free, quick, easy, graceful, not paddlefooted, or stiff in hip movements.

Temperament: Happy, alert and friendly. Neither shy nor aggressive.

Disqualifications: Height over 12 inches. An all-white dog or a dog with no white.

Approved June 10, 1991
Effective July 31, 1991

Meet the Pekingese

Recognized by AKC® in 1906
Pekingese Club of America (thepekingeseclubofamerica.net), formed in 1909

Traits
- Affectionate
- Regal Dignity
- Opinionated

Pekingese

AKC Official Guide to Toy Dogs

HISTORY

Chinese lore has it that the Pekingese was the lovely outcome of a romance between a lion and the tiny marmoset monkey. Fanciful tales aside, small short-muzzled dogs appear in Chinese art as far back as 200 BC, and DNA studies have confirmed their antiquity for at least two thousand years. By the early eighteenth century, these little dogs, also known as "lion dogs," were so prized among the Chinese aristocracy that it was a crime, punishable by death, to allow outsiders to obtain one. They remained a secret of the East until September 1860, when British troops stormed the Forbidden City. In the abandoned Summer Palace, British soldiers found the body of an elderly aunt of the Emperor surrounded by her five little dogs. The soldiers brought them back to England. One, appropriately named Lootie, was given to Queen Victoria and, as breeds favored by women sitting on British thrones are known to do, Pekingese soon became all the rage among not only British aristocracy but also America's rich and famous. They remain popular today as treasured companions and show dogs. In addition, some have been setting their tufted feet into other arenas, including obedience and agility. A few compete in these events in glorious full coat, which is always sure to please the crowds.

FORM AND FUNCTION

As pampered pets of the ladies of the imperial court, Pekingese had to be small enough to nestle in a lap, no heavier than 14 pounds. Smaller varieties, about 6 pounds, known as "sleeve dogs," were carried around in the oversized sleeves of traditional Chinese robes. Size notwithstanding, their image should be lionlike, conveying courage, dignity, and boldness. Their short bowed legs were designed to move slowly, so that they could not stray. It's a leisurely, soothing gait, designed to bring to mind a rowboat on a still lake, gently rocking back and forth. Their abundant hair, composed of a long straight outer coat and a soft, plush undercoat, comes in all colors, a must for their role as fashion accessory for their owners. As Dowager Empress Tzu Hsi wrote in her standard for the breed, penned in the late nineteenth century, Pekingese colors should be a golden sable to go with a yellow robe, or "the color of a red bear, or of a black bear, or a white bear, or striped like a dragon, So that there may be dogs appropriate to each of the Imperial robes."

LIVING WITH A PEKE

The ideal Pekingese owner is an emperor or empress, but since those are in short supply nowadays, ordinary people will do, especially those who thrive on huge amounts of love and attention. Pekes are affectionate, loving, and intelligent. They have a talent for making their owners feel like royalty. They develop strong connections to their people, sometimes to just one person. They typically regard their owners as if the sun rises and sets on their loving faces. Watch a Peke walking, on the street or in the show ring, and notice that the dog is constantly glancing upward, always checking to see whether his person is happy. Their thick double coats require a good deal of maintenance, a minimum of an hour of brushing each week.

Pekingese puppies appear to be covered in a short woolly coat, so there's no way, other than seeing the parents, to tell how their hair will grow. Some other traits to look for, especially in a show prospect, include a short back, open nostrils, and slightly turned-out feet. Gauged on the hands of a clock, the feet should be positioned at eleven and one. Most important is a friendly, outgoing, loving personality, a hallmark of the breed.

COMPETITION

Pekingese are eligible to compete in conformation, obedience, rally, agility, tracking, and coursing ability tests. Many Pekes are charismatic therapy dogs.

Official Standard for the Pekingese

General Appearance: The Pekingese is a well-balanced, compact dog of Chinese origin with a heavy front and lighter hindquarters. Its temperament is one of directness, independence and individuality. Its image is lionlike, implying courage, dignity, boldness and self-esteem rather than daintiness or delicacy.

Size, Substance, Proportion: *Size/Substance*—The Pekingese, when lifted, is surprisingly heavy for its size. It has a stocky, muscular body. All weights are correct within the limit of 14 pounds. Disqualification: Weight over 14 pounds. *Proportion*—Overall balance is of utmost importance. The head is large in proportion to the body. The Pekingese is slightly longer than tall when measured from the forechest to the buttocks. The overall outline is an approximate ratio of 3 high to 5 long.

Head: *Face*—The topskull is massive, broad and flat and, when combined with the wide set eyes, cheekbones and broad lower jaw, forms the correctly shaped face. When viewed from the front, the skull is wider than deep, which contributes to the desired rectangular, envelope-shaped appearance of the head. In profile, the face is flat. When viewed from the side, the chin, nose leather and brow all lie in one plane, which slants very slightly backward from chin to forehead. *Ears*—They are heart-shaped, set on the front corners of the topskull, and lie flat against the head. The leather does not extend below the jaw. Correctly placed ears, with their heavy feathering and long fringing, frame the sides of the face and add to the appearance of a wide, rectangular head. *Eyes*—They are large, very dark, round, lustrous and set wide apart. The look is bold, not bulging. The eye rims are black and the white of the eye does not show when the dog is looking straight ahead. *Nose*—It is broad, short and black. Nostrils are wide and open rather than pinched. A line drawn horizontally over the top of the nose intersects slightly above the center of the eyes. *Wrinkle*—It effectively separates the upper and lower areas of the face. It is a hair-covered fold of skin extending from one cheek over the bridge of the nose in a wide inverted V to the other cheek. It is never so prominent or heavy as to crowd the facial features, obscure more than a small portion of the eyes, or fall forward over any portion of the nose leather. *Stop*—It is obscured from view by the over-nose wrinkle. *Muzzle*—It is very flat, broad, and well filled-in below the eyes. The skin is black on all colors. Whiskers add to the desired expression. *Mouth*—The lower jaw is undershot and broad. The black lips meet neatly and neither teeth nor tongue show when the mouth is closed.

Neck, Body, Tail: *Neck*—It is very short and thick. *Body*—It is pear-shaped, compact and low to the ground. It is heavy in front with well-sprung ribs slung between the forelegs. The forechest is broad and full without a protruding breastbone. The underline rises from the deep chest to the lighter loin, thus forming a narrow waist. The topline is straight and the loin is short. *Tail*—The high-set tail is slightly arched and carried well over the back, free of kinks or curls. Long, profuse, straight fringing may fall to either side.

Forequarters: They are short, thick and heavy-boned. The bones of the forelegs are moderately bowed between the pastern and elbow. The broad chest, wide set forelegs and the closer rear legs all contribute to the correct rolling gait. The distance from the point of the shoulder to the tip of the withers is approximately equal to the distance from the point of the shoulder to the elbow. Shoulders are well laid back and fit smoothly onto the body. The elbows are always close to the body. Front feet are turned out slightly when standing or moving. The pasterns slope gently.

Hindquarters: They are lighter in bone than the forequarters. There is moderate angulation of stifle and hock. When viewed from behind, the rear legs are reasonably close and parallel, and the feet point straight ahead when standing or moving.

Coat and Presentation: *Coat*—It is a long, coarse-textured, straight, stand-off outer coat, with thick, soft undercoat. The coat forms a noticeable mane on the neck and shoulder area with the coat on the remainder of the body somewhat shorter in length. A long and profuse coat is desirable providing it does not obscure the shape of the body. Long feathering is found on toes, backs of the thighs and forelegs, with longer fringing on the ears and tail. *Presentation*—Presentation should accentuate the natural outline of the Pekingese. Any obvious trimming or sculpting of the coat, detracting from its natural appearance, should be severely penalized.

Color: All coat colors and markings are allowable and of equal merit. A black mask or a self-colored face is equally acceptable. Regardless of coat color the exposed skin of the muzzle, nose, lips and eye rims is black.

Gait: It is unhurried, dignified, free and strong, with a slight roll over the shoulders. This motion is smooth and effortless and is as free as possible from bouncing, prancing or jarring. The rolling gait results from a combination of the bowed forelegs, well laid back shoulders, full broad chest and narrow light rear, all of which produce adequate reach and moderate drive.

Temperament: A combination of regal dignity, intelligence and self-importance make for a good natured, opinionated and affectionate companion to those who have earned its respect.

Disqualification: Weight over 14 pounds.

The foregoing is a description of the ideal Pekingese. Any deviation should be penalized in direct proportion to the extent of that deviation.

Approved January 13, 2004
Effective March 2, 2004

Meet the Pomeranian

Recognized by AKC® in 1888
American Pomeranian Club (ampomclub.org), founded in 1900

Traits
- Vivacious Spirit
- Confident
- Inquisitive

HISTORY

In the Baltic region, there once existed a province called Pomerania that was bordered by Germany on one side and by what is now Poland on the other. Although spitz-type dogs were prevalent throughout the northern countryside of this territory, a specific smaller, perky dog of this type was being called the Pomeranian.

In the early days, Pomeranians were often seen riding alongside their masters on the boats of the local traders. They served as guard dogs on the boats and companions to the crews. Back at their homesteads, they were used as herders, cart pullers, and protectors of their families. Dogs of the spitz variety are depicted in artwork as early as 400 BC, but credit for the Pomeranian's international fame belongs to England. In the 1700s, Queen Charlotte acquired a dog of 20-plus pounds from the province of Pomerania, which was the first official entry of that type of dog into Great Britain. Queen Charlotte's granddaughter, Queen Victoria, made the breed fashionable in England in the 1880s.

In 1911, the first American Pomeranian Club specialty show was held in New York City at the Waldorf Astoria Hotel. The Pomeranian is still a dog very well suited to the conformation ring because of his self-possessed, "look at me" cocky nature.

FORM AND FUNCTION

Climate and outdoor work in their location of origin made it essential that these little dogs have harsh water- and snow-resistant coats. Double coats provided warmth while working outside during those long winter months. Prick ears enhanced hearing, and medium-sized dark eyes improved vision in the reflective glare of a snowy region. Their alert temperaments and sharp voices suited them for their work as guard dogs and herders.

Ideal type for this compact, short-backed, sturdy breed has evolved over the years. Their signature trait is the heavy stand-off double coat, which comes in a variety of colors. The shift in popularity of specific colors has been dramatic. It wasn't until 1914 that the first orange and orange-sable Poms came into favor. In the twenty-first century, orange and sable Poms comprise the largest number of show entries.

LIVING WITH A POM

In trying to decide whether this breed is right for your situation, there are certain things to keep in mind. Although bred for a variety of purposes centuries ago, the Pomeranian today is a companion dog. Poms thrive on attention and love getting involved in your life, in your cat's life, or in the life of the dog in the next yard. They love the companionship of other Pomeranians within the same household.

Although their personalities don't reflect it, Poms are fragile in many ways. Apart from the usual puppy safeguards, a young Pom must be particularly safeguarded against being dropped, falls, and head and neck injuries. If there are children in the home, this must be considered as a possible concern for the safety of the puppy.

Since these dogs are so small, their exercise needs are easily satisfied. Dashing around the apartment, a moderate afternoon walk, or laps around the fenced perimeter of the yard provides adequate exercise for these little darlings.

Owners interested in the Pomeranian must be willing and committed to the maintenance and basic care of the breed's notably glorious coat. Although it is a double coat and tends to naturally shed dirt and water, a large amount of brushing and bathing, as well as nail care and dental cleanings, are necessary to keep this breed in good condition and health.

COMPETITION

Although small in stature, the Pomeranian is a highly capable and an extremely willing and enthusiastic participant in most AKC® events. Their vivacious personality and optimistic nature make them excellent partners in performance events, as well as in conformation. Agility, obedience, rally, and even herding events are often in their repertoire of titles and achievements. Therapy work is another area in which they excel. Their loving personalities and basic intuition of human needs lend themselves fabulously to therapy work.

Official Standard for the Pomeranian

General Appearance: The Pomeranian is a compact, short-backed, active toy dog of Nordic descent. The double coat consists of a short dense undercoat with a profuse harsh-textured longer outer coat. The heavily plumed tail is one of the characteristics of the breed. It is set high and lies flat on the back. He is alert in character, exhibits intelligence in expression, is buoyant in deportment, and is inquisitive by nature. The Pomeranian is cocky, commanding, and animated as he gaits. He is sound in composition and action.

Size, Proportion, Substance: *Weight*—Is from 3 to 7 pounds with the ideal weight for show specimens being 4 to 6 pounds. Any dog over or under the limits is objectionable; however, overall quality should be favored over size. *Proportion*—The Pomeranian is a square breed with a short back. The ratio of body length to height at the withers being 1 to 1. These proportions are measured from the prosternum to the point of buttocks, and from the highest point of the withers to the ground. *Substance*—Sturdy, medium-boned.

Head: *Head*—In balance with the body, when viewed from above, broad at the back tapering to the nose to form a wedge. *Expression*—May be referred to as fox-like, denoting his alert and intelligent nature. *Eyes*—Dark, bright, medium sized, and almond shaped; set well into the skull with the width between the eyes balancing the other facial features. Eye rims are black, except self-colored in chocolate, beaver and blue. *Ears*—Small, mounted high and carried erect. Proper ear set should be favored over size. *Skull*—Closed, slightly round but not domed. *Stop*—Well pronounced. *Muzzle*—Rather short, straight, free of lippiness, neither coarse nor snipey. Ratio of length of muzzle to skull is $\frac{1}{3}$ to $\frac{2}{3}$. *Nose*—Pigment is black except self-colored in chocolate, beaver and blue. *Bite*—Scissors, one tooth out of alignment is acceptable. Major faults—Round, domed skull. Undershot, overshot or wry bite. Disqualification—Eye(s) light blue, blue marbled, blue flecked.

Neck, Topline, Body: *Neck*—Set well into the shoulders with sufficient length to allow the head to be carried proud and high. ***Topline***—Level from withers to croup. ***Body***—Compact and well-ribbed. ***Chest***—Oval tapered extending to the point of elbows with a pronounced prosternum. ***Back***—Short-coupled, straight and strong. ***Loin***—Short with slight tuck-up. Croup is flat. ***Tail***—Heavily plumed, set high and lies flat and straight on the back. Major fault—Low tail set.

Forequarters: ***Shoulders***—Well laid back. Shoulder blade and upper arm length are equal. ***Elbows***—Held close to the body and turn neither in nor out. ***Legs***—When viewed from the front are moderately spaced, straight and parallel to each other, set well behind the forechest. Height from withers to elbows approximately equals height from ground to elbow. Shoulders and legs are moderately muscled. ***Pasterns***—Straight and strong. ***Feet***—Round, tight, appearing cat-like, well-arched, compact, and turn neither in nor out, standing well up on toes. ***Dewclaws***—May be removed. Major fault—Down in pasterns.

Hindquarters: ***Hindquarters***—Angulation balances that of the forequarters. Buttocks are well behind the set of the tail. ***Thighs***—Moderately muscled. Upper thigh and lower leg length are equal. ***Stifles***—Strong, moderately bent and clearly defined. ***Legs***—When viewed from the rear straight and parallel to each other. ***Hocks***—When viewed from the side are perpendicular to the ground and strong. *Feet*—Same as forequarters. *Dewclaws*—May be removed. Major faults—Cowhocks, knees turning in or out or lack of soundness in legs or stifles.

Coat: The Pomeranian is a double-coated breed. The body should be well covered with a short, dense undercoat with long harsh-textured guard hair growing through, forming the longer abundant outer coat which stands off from the body. The coat should form a ruff around the neck, framing the head, extending over the shoulders and chest. Head and leg coat is tightly packed and shorter in length than that of the body. Forelegs are well-feathered. Thighs and hind legs are heavily coated to the hock forming a skirt. Tail is profusely covered with long, harsh spreading straight hair forming a plume. Females may not carry as thick or long a coat as a male. Puppy coat may be dense and shorter overall and may or may not show guard hair. A cotton-type coat is undesirable in an adult. Coat should be in good and healthy condition especially the skirt, tail, and undercarriage. Trimming for neatness and a clean outline is permissible. Major fault—Soft, flat or open coat.

Color: All colors, patterns, and variations thereof are allowed and must be judged on an equal basis.

Brindle: Dark cross stripes on any solid color or allowed pattern. *Parti*: White base with any solid color or allowed pattern. A white blaze is preferred on the head. Ticking is undesirable. *Extreme Piebald*: White with patches of color on head and base of tail. *Piebald*: White with patches of color on head, body, and base of tail. *Irish*: Color on the head and body with white legs, chest and collar. *Tan Points:* Any solid color or allowed pattern with markings sharply defined above each eye, inside the ears, muzzle, throat, forechest, all lower legs and feet, the underside of the tail and skirt. The richer the tan the more desirable. Tan markings should be readily visible.

Major fault—Distinct white on whole foot or on one or more whole feet (except white or parti) on any acceptable color or pattern.

Classifications—The Open Classes at specialty shows may be divided by color as follows: Open Red, Orange, Cream, and Sable; Open Black, Brown, and Blue; Open Any Other Color, Pattern, or Variation.

Gait: The Pomeranian's movement has good reach in the forequarters and strong drive with the hindquarters, displaying efficient, ground covering movement that should never be viewed as ineffective or busy. Head carriage should remain high and proud with the overall outline maintained. Gait is smooth, free, balanced and brisk. When viewed from the front and rear while moving at a walk or slow trot the Pomeranian should double track, but as the speed increases the legs converge slightly towards a center line. The forelegs and hind legs are carried straight forward, with neither elbows nor stifles turned in nor out. The topline should remain firm and level with the overall balance maintained.

Temperament: The Pomeranian is an extrovert, exhibiting great intelligence and a vivacious spirit, making him a great companion dog as well as a competitive show dog. Even though a toy dog, the Pomeranian must be subject to the same requirements of soundness and structure prescribed for all breeds, and any deviation from the ideal described in the standard should be penalized to the extent of the deviation.

Disqualifications: Eye(s) light blue, blue marbled, blue flecked.

Approved July 12, 2011
Effective August 31, 2011

Meet the Poodle (Toy)

Recognized by AKC® in 1887
Poodle Club of America (poodleclubofamerica.org), formed in 1931

Traits
- Self-Confident
- Elegant
- Intelligent

HISTORY

Since history documents the Poodle in various parts of the world, there is some doubt as to the land of its origin. The breed is supposed to have originated in Germany, where it is known as the Pudel. For years, it has been regarded as the national dog of France, where it was commonly used as a retriever and traveling trick or circus dog. In France, it was known as the Caniche, which translates as "duck dog." The English word poodle comes from the German pudel or pudelin, meaning "to splash in the water." The expression "French Poodle" in all probability is a result of the dog's popularity in France.

The Poodle's use as a water retriever is how his unique trim, although becoming more stylized over time, developed. Portions of the Poodle's coat were clipped to help facilitate movement in swimming. There is a purpose to every sculpted form; for example, the mane to protect heart and lungs, the rosettes to protect kidneys, the puffs to protect joints, and the tail to propel the dog like a rudder. The coat is dense and curly, long enough to freeze on top and remain warm and dry near the skin in cold weather.

FORM AND FUNCTION

Although they are one breed, Poodles come in three varieties or sizes: Toy (10 inches from shoulder to floor), Miniature (15 inches), and Standard (over 15 inches). In accordance with present-day show classification, there is an array of colors to suit almost anyone's taste. Any solid color is allowed: white, black, brown, café-au-lait, cream, blue, apricot, red, silver, and gray. Parti-colors are discouraged and disqualified from conformation competition.

The Poodle should have a dark oval eye (large protruding eyes could be damaged while working in marsh grasses or rough water), and the head is streamlined for getting through sharp marsh grasses and for water diving. The muzzle is long, strong, and tight-lipped, with no open flews or pendulous lips, to eliminate the possibility of choking or drowning when delivering a struggling bird through the water. Poodle ears are long and low-set to protect them in water.

LIVING WITH A TOY POODLE

The combination of intelligence, a loyal, courageous, spirited temperament, and the appearance of power and elegance has kept the Poodle a popular household companion for decades. When considering obtaining a puppy, a strong healthy dog with excellent temperament should be the primary goal. The difference between a show-quality and a pet-quality puppy obtained from a good breeder may be so minute that only a trained eye can make a distinction. Such differences may only be a minor fault that prevents the puppy from qualifying for the show ring, something as simple as a variation in eye color, a coat lacking in texture, or an improper bite. These traits in no way affect the puppy's ability to be a great companion.

The Poodle's nonshedding coat makes him a good dog for people with allergies. Poodles must be groomed on a regular schedule. The pet Poodle doesn't have to be fancy, just bathed, brushed, and trimmed regularly. Poodles are very people-oriented and must be an integral part of their owner's life to be happy.

COMPETITION

Poodles are extremely intelligent and love to be trained, so they excel in all kinds of sports. They are crowd-pleasing knockouts in the conformation ring and their brains and trainability give them an edge in obedience and agility. Many Toy Poodles make outstanding therapy dogs.

Official Standard for the Poodle

The Standard for the Poodle (Toy variety) is the same as for the Standard and Miniature varieties except as regards heights.

General Appearance: *Carriage and Condition*—That of a very active, intelligent and elegant-appearing dog, squarely built, well proportioned, moving soundly and carrying himself proudly. Properly clipped in the traditional fashion and carefully groomed, the Poodle has about him an air of distinction and dignity peculiar to himself.

Size, Proportion, Substance: Size—*The Standard Poodle* is over 15 inches at the highest point of the shoulders. Any Poodle which is 15 inches or less in height shall be disqualified from competition as a Standard Poodle.

The Miniature Poodle is 15 inches or under at the highest point of the shoulders, with a minimum height in excess of 10 inches. Any Poodle which is over 15 inches or is 10 inches or less at the highest point of the shoulders shall be disqualified from competition as a Miniature Poodle.

The Toy Poodle is 10 inches or under at the highest point of the shoulders. Any Poodle which is more than 10 inches at the highest point of the shoulders shall be disqualified from competition as a Toy Poodle.

As long as the Toy Poodle is definitely a Toy Poodle, and the Miniature Poodle a Miniature Poodle, both in balance and proportion for the Variety, diminutiveness shall be the deciding factor when all other points are equal.

Proportion—To ensure the desirable squarely built appearance, the length of body measured from the breastbone to the point of the rump approximates the height from the highest point of the shoulders to the ground.

Substance—Bone and muscle of both forelegs and hindlegs are in proportion to size of dog.

Head and Expression: *(a) Eyes*—Very dark, oval in shape and set far enough apart and positioned to create an alert intelligent expression. Major fault: eyes round, protruding, large or very light.

(b) Ears—Hanging close to the head, set at or slightly below eye level. The ear leather is long, wide and thickly feathered; however, the ear fringe should not be of excessive length.

(c) Skull—Moderately rounded, with a slight but definite stop. Cheekbones and muscles flat. Length from occiput to stop about the same as length of muzzle. *(d) Muzzle*—Long, straight and fine, with slight chiseling under the eyes. Strong without lippiness. The chin definite enough to preclude snipiness. Major fault: Lack of chin. *Teeth*—White,

strong and with a scissors bite. Major fault: Undershot, overshot, wry mouth.

Neck, Topline, Body: *Neck* well proportioned, strong and long enough to permit the head to be carried high and with dignity. Skin snug at throat. The neck rises from strong, smoothly muscled shoulders. Major fault: Ewe neck. The *topline* is level, neither sloping nor roached, from the highest point of the shoulder blade to the base of the tail, with the exception of a slight hollow just behind the shoulder. **Body** *(a)* Chest deep and moderately wide with well sprung ribs. *(b)* The loin is short, broad and muscular. *(c)* Tail straight, set on high and carried up, docked of sufficient length to insure a balanced outline. Major fault: Set low, curled, or carried over the back.

Forequarters: Strong, smoothly muscled shoulders. The shoulder blade is well laid back and approximately the same length as the upper foreleg. Major fault: Steep shoulder.

Forelegs—Straight and parallel when viewed from the front. When viewed from the side the elbow is directly below the highest point of the shoulder. The pasterns are strong. Dewclaws may be removed.

Feet—The feet are rather small, oval in shape with toes well arched and cushioned on thick firm pads. Nails short but not excessively shortened. The feet turn neither in nor out. Major fault: Paper or splay foot.

Hindquarters: The angulation of the hindquarters balances that of the forequarters.

Hind legs straight and parallel when viewed from the rear. Muscular with width in the region of the stifles which are well bent; femur and tibia are about equal in length; hock to heel short and perpendicular to the ground. When standing, the rear toes are only slightly behind the point of the rump. Major fault: Cow-hocks.

Value of Points	
General appearance, temperament, carriage and condition	30
Head, expression, ears, eyes and teeth	20
Body, neck, legs, feet and tail	20
Gait	20
Coat, color and texture	10

Coat: *(a) Quality*—(1) Curly: of naturally harsh texture, dense throughout. (2) Corded: hanging in tight even cords of varying length; longer on mane or body coat, head, and ears; shorter on puffs, bracelets, and pompons.

(b) Clip—A Poodle under twelve months may be shown in the "Puppy" clip. In all regular classes, Poodles twelve months or over must be shown in the "English Saddle" or "Continental" clip. In the Stud Dog and Brood Bitch classes and in a non-competitive Parade of Champions, Poodles may be shown in the "Sporting" clip. A Poodle shown in any other type of clip shall be disqualified. (1) "Puppy"—A Poodle under a year old may be shown in the "Puppy" clip with the coat long. The face, throat, feet and base of the tail are shaved. The entire shaven foot is visible. There is a pompon on the end of the tail. In order to give a neat appearance and a smooth unbroken line, shaping of the coat is permissible. (2) "English Saddle"—In the "English Saddle" clip, the face, throat, feet, forelegs and base of the tail are shaved, leaving puffs on the forelegs and a pompon on the end of the tail. The hindquarters are covered with a short blanket of hair except for a curved shaved area on each flank and two shaved bands on each hindleg. The entire shaven foot and a portion of the shaven leg above the puff are visible. The rest of the body is left in full coat but may be shaped in order to insure overall balance. (3) "Continental"—In the "Continental" clip, the face, throat, feet, and base of the tail are shaved. The hindquarters are shaved with pompons (optional) on the hips. The legs are shaved, leaving bracelets on the hindlegs and puffs on the forelegs. There is a pompon on the end of the tail. The entire shaven foot and a portion of the shaven foreleg above the puff are visible. The rest of the body is left in full coat but may be shaped in order to insure overall balance. (4) "Sporting"—In the "Sporting" clip, a Poodle shall be shown with face, feet, throat, and base of tail shaved, leaving a scissored cap on the top of the head and a pompon on the end of the tail. The rest of the body and legs are clipped or scissored to follow the outline of the dog leaving a short blanket of coat no longer than 1 inch in length. The hair on the legs may be slightly longer than that on the body.

In all clips the hair of the topknot may be left free or held in place by elastic bands. The hair is only of sufficient length to present a smooth outline. "Topknot" refers only to hair on the skull, from stop to occiput. This is the only area where elastic bands may be used.

Color: The coat is an even and solid color at the skin. In blues, grays, silvers, browns, cafe-au-laits, apricots and creams the coat may show varying shades of the same color. This is frequently present in the somewhat darker feathering of the ears and in the tipping of the ruff. While clear colors are definitely preferred, such natural variation in the shading of the coat is not to be considered a fault. Brown and cafe-au-lait Poodles have liver-colored noses, eye-rims and lips, dark toenails and dark amber eyes. Black, blue, gray, silver, cream and white Poodles have black noses, eye-rims and lips, black or self colored toenails and very dark eyes. In the apricots while the foregoing coloring is preferred, liver-colored noses, eye-rims and lips, and amber eyes are permitted but are not desirable. Major fault: Color of nose, lips and eye-rims incomplete, or of wrong color for color of dog.

Parti-colored dogs shall be disqualified. The coat of a parti-colored dog is not an even solid color at the skin but is of two or more colors.

Gait: A straightforward trot with light springy action and strong hindquarters drive. Head and tail carried up. Sound effortless movement is essential.

Temperament: Carrying himself proudly, very active, intelligent, the Poodle has about him an air of distinction and dignity peculiar to himself. Major fault: Shyness or sharpness.

Major Faults: Any distinct deviation from the desired characteristics described in the breed standard.

Disqualifications: *Size*—A dog over or under the height limits specified shall be disqualified. *Clip*—A dog in any type of clip other than those listed under coat shall be disqualified. *Parti-colors*—The coat of a parti-colored dog is not an even solid color at the skin but of two or more colors. Parti-colored dogs shall be disqualified.

Approved August 14, 1984
Reformatted March 27, 1990

Meet the Pug

Recognized by AKC® in 1885
Pug Dog Club of America (www.pugdogclubofamerica.com), formed in 1931

Traits
- Mischievous
- Charming
- Outgoing

HISTORY

The Pug is of Chinese origin and dates back to the pre-Christian era. They were prized possessions of the emperors of China and lived in a most luxurious atmosphere, at times even guarded by soldiers. Dutch traders brought Pugs from the East to Holland and on to England. The more robust cobby Pug we know today must be credited to English breeders. This happy little dog was enjoyed by many monarchs of Europe and to this day remains a favorite with royalty and discerning people all over the world.

The American Kennel Club® first recognized the breed in 1885. Their popularity has grown and, in recent years, has been boosted by their roles in several movies.

FORM AND FUNCTION

Standing between 10 and 13 inches and weighing about 14 to 18 pounds, this square dog is the largest of the toys. His tightly curled tail; unique head shape and facial features; short, blunt, square muzzle; and large, dark, round eyes give the Pug an expression that brings a smile to human faces.

LIVING WITH A PUG

When picking out a puppy, a new owner should look for nice clear eyes, wide open nostrils, and a robust personality. Pugs do not have many health problems, but they do shed year 'round. Their large round eyes are prone to injury from rosebushes, shrubs, etc., so you should be careful and check your yard. Pugs are susceptible to excessive heat just as humans are. If it feels hot for you, then it's hot for the Pug. Pugs love air-conditioning.

A Pug is anxious to please, anxious to learn, and anxious to love. His biggest requirement is that you love him back. The Pug has been bred to be a companion and a pleasure to his owners. He has an even temperament, exhibiting stability, playfulness, great charm, dignity, and an outgoing, loving disposition. He is extremely adaptable to his environment. If you want a Pug to run a 5-K with you, he will. If you want a Pug to just snuggle on your lap watching Men in Black, he will. No other dog can equal the Pug in his virtues as a family pet. He appeals to moms because of his natural cleanliness, intelligence, and for his toy size. He appeals to dads because he is a husky, sturdy dog with very little upkeep, needing no professional grooming. Children adore Pugs, and Pugs adore children. They are sturdy enough for fun and games. Older persons and shut-ins find them perfect as companions, too, because their greatest need is to be by your side and accepted into your way of life.

COMPETITION

Pugs have made a strong showing in conformation and do well in companion events like obedience, rally, and agility. They compete at all levels very confidently. When starting with a Pug, you can be sure to have many laughs and lots of fun.

Official Standard for the Pug

General Appearance: Symmetry and general appearance are decidedly square and cobby. A lean, leggy Pug and a dog with short legs and a long body are equally objectionable.

Size, Proportion, Substance: The Pug should be multum in parvo, and this condensation (if the word may be used) is shown by compactness of form, well knit proportions, and hardness of developed muscle. Weight from 14 to 18 pounds (dog or bitch) desirable. Proportion square.

Head: The head is large, massive, round—not apple-headed, with no indentation of the skull. The eyes are dark in color, very large, bold and prominent, globular in shape, soft and solicitous in expression, very lustrous, and, when excited, full of fire. The ears are thin, small, soft, like black velvet. There are two kinds—the "rose" and the "button." Preference is given to the latter. The wrinkles are large and deep. The muzzle is short, blunt, square, but not upfaced. Bite—A Pug's bite should be very slightly undershot.

Neck, Topline, Body: The neck is slightly arched. It is strong, thick, and with enough length to carry the head proudly. The short back is level from the withers to the high tail set. The body is short and cobby, wide in chest and well ribbed up. The tail is curled as tightly as possible over the hip. The double curl is perfection.

Forequarters: The legs are very strong, straight, of moderate length, and are set well under. The elbows should be directly under the withers when viewed from the side. The shoulders are moderately laid back. The pasterns are strong, neither steep nor down. The feet are neither so long as the foot of the hare, nor so round as that of the cat; well split-up toes, and the nails black. Dewclaws are generally removed.

Hindquarters: The strong, powerful hindquarters have moderate bend of stifle and short hocks perpendicular to the ground. The legs are parallel when viewed from behind. The hindquarters are in balance with the forequarters. The thighs and buttocks are full and muscular. Feet as in front.

Coat: The coat is fine, smooth, soft, short and glossy, neither hard nor woolly.

Color: The colors are fawn or black. The fawn color should be decided so as to make the contrast complete between the color and the trace and mask.

Markings: The markings are clearly defined. The muzzle or mask, ears, moles on cheeks, thumb mark or diamond on forehead, and the back trace should be as black as possible. The mask should be black. The more intense and well defined it is, the better. The trace is a black line extending from the occiput to the tail.

Gait: Viewed from the front, the forelegs should be carried well forward, showing no weakness in the pasterns, the paws landing squarely with the central toes straight ahead. The rear action should be strong and free through hocks and stifles, with no twisting or turning in or out at the joints. The hind legs should follow in line with the front. There is a slight natural convergence of the limbs both fore and aft. A slight roll of the hindquarters typifies the gait which should be free, self-assured, and jaunty.

Temperament: This is an even-tempered breed, exhibiting stability, playfulness, great charm, dignity, and an outgoing, loving disposition.

Disqualification: Any color other than fawn or black.

Approved April 8, 2008
Effective June 3, 2008

Meet the Russian Toy

Recognized by AKC® in 2022
Russian Toy Club of America (russiantoyclub.org), formed in 2011

Traits
- Loyal
- Impish
- Intelligent

HISTORY

One of dogdom's tiniest breeds, the Russian Toy descends from English Toy Terriers and boasts a connection to royalty. These elegant and lively dogs sporting both semi-long and short coats were brought to Russia from England in the eighteenth century to serve as prized companions of Russian aristocracy. The small breed performed the dual purpose of being living accessories at social gatherings and being hand warmers when carried in a muff. A long-coated black-and-tan type dog appeared in nineteenth-century Russian portraits and in 1907 at dog shows in St. Petersburg. Following the Russian Revolution of 1917, breeding these dogs was forbidden. The long coat nearly disappeared despite breeders' attempts to preserve the Russian-type terrier secretly. Fifty years later, the smooth-coated variety became known as the Russian Toy Terrier, and the long-coated type was called the Moscow Long-Coated Toy Terrier. In 1988, Russian breeders developed a new breed standard combining the two varieties as a single breed—the Russian (Russkiy) Toy Terrier. "Terrier" was later dropped, and the breed is known today as the Russian Toy. The breed was given Toy Group designation and became eligible for full AKC® recognition in 2022.

FORM AND FUNCTION

The Russian Toy thrives as a lap-loving companion with a caring and cheerful nature. Weighing in at less than 6½ pounds and measuring no taller than 11 inches from the ground to the top of the shoulders, this dog is tailor-made for cuddling and ride-sharing. The breed's diminutive stature, keen expression, and sleek body are often mistaken for a Chihuahua's. The Russian Toy's leggy silhouette and small head are this breed's standout features, which give the dogs the appearance of a small deer. A ruff on the chest and silky feathering on the forelegs and rear legs, sabre tail, and ears add distinction to the long-coated Russian Toys. Long-coated adult hair ranges from 1 to 3 inches long and needs a year to fill in. The full fringe takes three years to develop. A smooth coat feels soft and sleek and is close-lying. Breed colors include black and tan, brown and tan, blue and tan, red, sable, and brown sable.

LIVING WITH A RUSSIAN TOY

The Russian Toy's impish, larger-than-life personality entertains its owners. While some of these dogs happily keep busy playing with toys, running through the yard chasing squirrels, and barking at strangers, others opt for lounging the day away. The Russian

AKC Official Guide to Toy Dogs

Toy is loyal to family members and other people he knows and aloof around strangers. Both coat types are low maintenance, but the fringe requires weekly brushing. Monthly bathing will keep both types of coat shiny and free from dry skin and dead hair. Daily tooth-brushing and regular veterinary dental care will reduce periodontal disease, which begins in the first year.

COMPETITION

Russian Toys are eligible to compete in conformation, agility, obedience, tracking, and rally. They also excel in Fast CAT®, Trick Dog™, Scent Work, and the Canine Good Citizen® program. When well-socialized, these dogs might enjoy therapy work.

Official Standard for the Russian Toy

General Appearance: A small elegant dog, lively, long-legged, with fine bone and lean muscles. Sexual dimorphism only slightly defined. Active, cheerful, possessing keen intelligence, slightly aloof to strangers but neither cowardly nor aggressive.

Size, Proportion, Substance: The Russian Toy has a square build; the height, when measured vertically from the ground to the highest point of the withers, is equal to the length, when measured horizontally from the prosternum to the point of the buttocks. The height at the elbows is only slightly more than half of the height at withers. The chest is sufficiently deep reaching to the elbow. Height at withers for both dogs and bitches: 8 inches to 11 inches.

Weight for both dogs and bitches: up to 6½ pounds. Disqualifications—Height at withers over 12 inches or under 7 inches. Weight less than 2 pounds.

Head: The *head* is small compared to the body. *Expression*—The expression is bright, attentive with attitude. *Eyes* are quite large, rounded, dark, slightly prominent, set well apart and looking straight ahead. Eyelids are tightly fitting. Black and Tan dogs have eyes that are darkest brown to black with black eye rims. Chocolate and Tan dogs have eyes that are brown to light brown and eye rims that are brown to light brown (darker color preferred). Blue and Tan dogs have eyes and eye rims that are slate grey. Red coated dogs have eyes that are darkest brown to black with black eye rims. Red Sable dogs have eyes that are darkest brown to black with black eye rims. Red Brown dogs have eyes and eye rims that are brown (darker color preferred). *Ears*—Ears are big, thin, set high, erect and wider at the base tapering to a triangular shape. Semi-pricked ears in longhaired dogs with heavy fringes is permissible but not desirable.

Disqualification: Hanging (completely down) ears. *Skull*—The skull is high but not too wide (width at the level of zygomatic arches does not exceed the depth of the skull). *Stop*—The stop is clearly pronounced. *Muzzle*—The muzzle is lean and tapered and is slightly shorter than the skull. Cheekbones—The cheekbones are only slightly pronounced. Nose—Black and Tan dogs have black noses. Chocolate and Tan dogs have noses that are brown to light brown (darker color preferred). Blue and Tan dogs have slate grey noses. Red coated dogs have black noses. Red Sable dogs have black noses. Red Brown dogs have brown noses (darker color preferred). *Lips*—Lips are thin, lean, tight-fitting. Black and Tan dogs have black lips. Chocolate and Tan dogs have lips that are brown to light brown (darker color preferred). Blue and Tan dogs have slate grey lips. Red coated dogs have black lips. Red Sable dogs have black lips. Red Brown dogs have brown lips (darker color preferred). *Bite*—The teeth should meet in a scissor bite.

Russian Toy teeth are small, white. Absence of two incisors is permitted in each jaw. Faults—Level bite or incisors sloping forward. The absence of more than two incisors in either jaw is a serious fault. Disqualifications—Overshot, undershot. Absence of one canine.

Neck, Topline, Body: *Neck*—The neck is long, lean, carried high, slightly arched. *Topline*—The topline gradually slopes from the withers to the root of the tail. Withers—The withers are slightly pronounced. *Body*—The chest is oval, sufficiently deep and not too wide. Underline—The underline has a tucked up belly and drawn up flanks, forming a nicely curved line from the chest to the flanks. Back—The back is strong and straight. Loin—The loin is short and slightly arched. Croup—The croup is somewhat rounded and slightly sloping. *Tail*—Tails may be natural or docked (only two or three vertebrae are left), and is carried high. The undocked (natural) tail is a sickle tail. The tail

Russian Toy

should not be carried lower than back level when moving. Fault—Low set tail.

Forequarters: Shoulders—The shoulder blades are moderately long and not too sloping. Upper Arm—The upper arm forms an angle of 105 degrees with the shoulder blade. The length of upper arm is approximately equal to the length of shoulder. Elbow—The elbow is in line with the body. Legs—Forequarters legs are thin and lean. Seen from the front, the front legs are straight and parallel. The forearm is long, straight. The carpus (wrist) is lean. Pasterns are almost vertical. Dewclaws may be removed or left natural. Feet and Toes—Forefeet are small, oval, turning neither in nor out with pads that are cushioned. Toes are well knit and arched.

Hind feet are a little bit narrower than forefeet with pads that are cushioned and toes are well knit and arched. Pads and Nails—Black and Tan dogs have black nails and pads. Chocolate and Tan dogs have nails and pads that are brown to light brown (darker color preferred). Blue and Tan dogs have slate grey nails and pads. Red coated dogs have black nails and pads. Red Sable dogs have black nails and pads. Red Brown dogs have brown nails and pads (darker color preferred).

Hindquarters: Seen from the rear, the hind legs are straight and parallel, but standing a little bit wider than the forelegs. Stifles and hocks are sufficiently bent. Angulation—Hindquarters should be sufficiently angulated. The upper thigh muscles are lean and developed. The upper and lower thighs are of the same length. Hocks should be vertical. There should be no rear dewclaws. Serious fault—Short legs.

Skin: The skin should be dry and tight-fitting.

Coat: Hair—There exists two types for the breed: smooth-coated and long-coated. Smooth coat dogs have short, close-lying, shiny hair, without undercoat or bald patches. Long coat dogs have bodies covered with moderately long (one inch to three inches) straight or slightly wavy hair, close-lying, which does not hide the natural outline of the body. Hair on the head and on the front part of limbs is short and close-lying. There are distinct feathers on rear side of limbs. The feet have long, silky hair which completely hides the nails. Long coated dogs have ears that are covered with thick, long hair forming a fringe. Dogs of more than three years have such a fringe which should completely hide the outer edges and tips of the ears. Body hair should not look tousled nor be too short (less than ½ inch). Disqualification—Long coat dogs: absence of any fringes on ears and presence of curly hair. (Dogs younger than 18 months may have sparse or few fringes).

Color: Russian Toy coats may be Black and Tan, Chocolate and Tan, Blue and Tan, Red, Red Sable, or Red Brown. Black and Tan coats are jet black with rich, bright tan markings over eyes, on cheeks, inside ears, on chest, legs, and on underside of tail. Chocolate and Tan coats are rich chocolate brown with tan markings over eyes, on cheeks, inside ears, on chest, legs, and on underside of tail. Blue and Tan coats are blue based grey coloring with tan markings over eyes, on cheeks, inside ears, on chest, legs, and on underside of tail. Red coats are whole-colored red that may range from rich ruby to lighter hues, but deeper saturated color is preferred. Red Sable coats are red with black-tipped hair on body and ears. Red Brown coats are red with brown-tipped hair on body and ears. Faults—Presence of bald patches in smooth coat dogs. Too long or too short hair on body of long coat dogs. Small white spots under ½ inch on chest and toes. Solid black, brown and blue colors. Tan markings too large or with dark shadings. Any white spots on the head, abdomen and above metacarpus. Severe fault—Large white patches over ½ inch on chest and throat. Disqualification—Presence of brindle markings.

Gait: Easy, straightforward, fast. No noticeable change in the topline when moving. Temperament: Active, cheerful, possessing keen intelligence, slightly aloof to strangers but neither cowardly nor aggressive. Fault—Timid behavior.

Faults: Any departure from the foregoing points should be considered a fault and the seriousness with which the fault should be regarded should be in exact proportion to its degree and its effect upon the health and welfare of the dog.

Disqualifications

Height at withers over 12 inches or under 7 inches.
Weight less than 2 pounds.
Hanging (completely down) ears.
Overshot, undershot.
Absence of one canine.
Long coat dogs: absence of any fringes on ears and presence of curly hair. (Dogs younger than 18 months may have sparse or few fringes.)
Presence of brindle markings.

Approved July 14, 2017
Effective June 27, 2018

Meet the Shih Tzu

Recognized by AKC® in 1969
American Shih Tzu Club (americanshihtzuclub.org/), formed in 1963

Traits
- Affectionate
- Outgoing
- Adaptable

HISTORY

Although its origins are shrouded in mystery, the Shih Tzu was probably one of a number of lionlike small dogs associated with the spread of Buddhism from India to Tibet; in fact, Shih Tzu means "lion." After being sent to the Chinese emperors as tribute, early Shih Tzu may have been crossed with such similar breeds as the Pekingese, Pug, and Japanese Chin. The distinctive breed we know today evolved mostly under the Qing (Ch'ing) Dowager Empress Tzu Hsi (1835–1908).

The Shih Tzu was highly prized as a companion in the royal court and was almost impossible to acquire for export. Fine specimens, often trimmed to resemble lions, appeared on scrolls and tapestries. The breed became extinct in China after the 1949 Communist Revolution because of its association with wealth and privilege. Therefore, modern Shih Tzu trace back to just six dogs and seven bitches brought to England and Scandinavia by diplomats stationed in China (not to mention a black and white Pekingese deliberately crossed with a Shih Tzu in England in 1952). The breed was admitted into the Miscellaneous Class in 1955, and it gained full recognition in 1969. After recognition, it swiftly became one of the most popular breeds in the United States.

FORM AND FUNCTION

Today's Shih Tzu, like his Chinese ancestors, makes an ideal pet. While the breed standard allows for considerable size variation, a proper Shih Tzu should always carry good weight and substance. This small, sturdy breed is a big dog in a little package, small enough for apartment life but athletic enough to enjoy a good walk or a romp in a fenced-in yard. As befits its noble ancestry, the Shih Tzu is proud of bearing, with a distinctively arrogant carriage. His unique "warm, sweet, wide-eyed, friendly and trusting" expression reflects his affectionate temperament. Another distinctive characteristic is the breed's long and luxurious double coat, which comes in a wide variety of colors and markings that were once prized by the palace eunuchs who were charged to care for these imperial pets.

LIVING WITH A SHIH TZU

A Shih Tzu is very adaptable and not at all high-strung. His main goal in life is to please you. If you want to play, your Shih Tzu will be eager to join in the game. If you are busy, he will sleep or amuse himself. Everyone, large and small, canine and human, is a friend. In fact, a burglar might receive a guided tour. Nevertheless, Shih Tzu can sometimes be stubborn and may try to charm and kiss their way out of being groomed or trained. Use generous praise and positive reinforcement rather than making training a battle of wills. Be firm but calm, and always end on a positive note.

The ideal owner will give his or her Shih Tzu lots of love. Shih Tzu puppies, particularly, seem to always be underfoot and can easily squirm out of someone's arms, so they may not do well in a home with very young children. Regular grooming is a must, even if you choose to keep your pet cut down or have him styled by a groomer.

While generally a healthy and long-lived breed, the Shih Tzu is more prone to eye and ear problems than some other breeds because of his large eyes, short muzzle, and drop ears. Shih Tzu puppies often bubble and snort while teething; if this problem persists or is very severe, seek veterinary attention. Young or old, Shih Tzu do not tolerate heat well and are not good swimmers. Allergies may also be an issue.

COMPETITION

The Shih Tzu's calm, affectionate nature makes him an ideal therapy dog. Some owners enjoy performance activities such as obedience, rally, and agility. Shih Tzu may not always be the speediest competitors, but they are very smart and have a great time—often in attention-getting ways that make spectators laugh! After all, why can't "down" mean hurl yourself onto your back, enthusiastically wag your entire body, and kiss the air?

Official Standard for the Shih Tzu

General Appearance: The Shih Tzu is a sturdy, lively, alert toy dog with long flowing double coat. Befitting his noble Chinese ancestry as a highly valued, prized companion and palace pet, the Shih Tzu is proud of bearing, has a distinctively arrogant carriage with head well up and tail curved over the back. Although there has always been considerable size variation, the Shih Tzu must be compact, solid, carrying good weight and substance.

Even though a toy dog, the Shih Tzu must be subject to the same requirements of soundness and structure prescribed for all breeds, and any deviation from the ideal described in the standard should be penalized to the extent of the deviation. Structural faults common to all breeds are as undesirable in the Shih Tzu as in any other breed, regardless of whether or not such faults are specifically mentioned in the standard.

Size, Proportion, Substance: *Size*—Ideally, height at withers is 9 to 10½ inches; but, not less than 8 inches nor more than 11 inches. Ideally, weight of mature dogs, 9 to 16 pounds. *Proportion*—Length between withers and root of tail is slightly longer than height at withers. The Shih Tzu must never be so high stationed as to appear leggy, nor so low stationed as to appear dumpy or squatty. *Substance*—Regardless of size, the Shih Tzu is always compact, solid and carries good weight and substance.

Head: *Head*—Round, broad, wide between eyes, its size in balance with the overall size of dog being neither too large nor too small. Fault: Narrow head, close-set eyes. *Expression*—Warm, sweet, wide-eyed, friendly and trusting. An overall well-balanced and pleasant expression supersedes the importance of individual parts. Care should be taken to look and examine well beyond the hair to determine if what is seen is the actual head and expression rather than an image created by grooming technique. *Eyes*—Large, round, not prominent, placed well apart, looking straight ahead. Very dark. Lighter on liver pigmented dogs and blue pigmented dogs. Fault: Small, close-set or light eyes; excessive eye white. ***Ears***—Large, set slightly below crown of skull; heavily coated. ***Skull***—Domed. ***Stop***—There is a definite stop. ***Muzzle***—Square, short, unwrinkled, with good cushioning, set no lower than bottom eye rim; never downturned. Ideally, no longer than 1 inch from tip of nose to stop, although length may vary slightly in relation to overall size of dog. Front of muzzle should be flat; lower lip and chin not protruding and definitely never receding. Fault: Snipiness, lack of definite stop. ***Nose***—Nostrils are broad, wide, and open. ***Pigmentation***—Nose, lips, eye rims are black on all colors, except liver on liver pigmented dogs and blue on blue pigmented dogs. Fault: Pink on nose, lips, or eye rims. ***Bite***—Undershot. Jaw is broad and wide. A missing tooth or slightly misaligned teeth should not be too severely penalized. Teeth and tongue should not show when mouth is closed. Fault: Overshot bite.

Neck, Topline, Body: Of utmost importance is an overall well-balanced dog with no exaggerated features. ***Neck***—Well set-on flowing smoothly into shoulders; of sufficient length to permit natural high head carriage and in balance with height and length of dog. ***Topline***—Level. ***Body***—Short-coupled and sturdy with no waist or tuck-up. The Shih Tzu is slightly longer than tall. Fault: Legginess. ***Chest***—Broad and deep with good spring-of-rib, however, not barrel-chested. Depth of ribcage should extend to just below elbow. Distance from elbow to withers is a little greater than from elbow to ground. ***Croup***—Flat. ***Tail***—Set on high, heavily plumed, carried in curve well over back. Too loose, too tight, too flat, or too low set a tail is undesirable and should be penalized to extent of deviation.

Forequarters: ***Shoulders***—Well-angulated, well laid-back, well laid-in, fitting smoothly into body. ***Legs***—Straight, well-boned, muscular, set well-apart and under chest, with elbows set close to body. ***Pasterns***—Strong, perpendicular. ***Dewclaws***—May be removed. ***Feet***—Firm, well-padded, point straight ahead.

Hindquarters: Angulation of hindquarters should be in balance with forequarters. ***Legs***—Well-boned, muscular, and straight when viewed from rear with well-bent stifles, not close set but in line with forequarters. ***Hocks***—Well let down, perpendicular. *Fault:* Hyperextension of hocks. ***Dewclaws***—May be removed. ***Feet***—Firm, well-padded, point straight ahead.

Coat: ***Coat***—Luxurious, double-coated, dense, long, and flowing. Slight wave permissible. Hair on top of head is tied up. Fault: Sparse coat, single coat, curly coat. ***Trimming***—Feet, bottom of coat, and anus may be done for neatness and to facilitate movement. Fault: Excessive trimming.

Color and Markings: All are permissible and to be considered equally.

Gait: The Shih Tzu moves straight and must be shown at its own natural speed, neither raced nor strung-up, to evaluate its smooth, flowing, effortless movement with good front reach and equally strong rear drive, level topline, naturally high head carriage, and tail carried in gentle curve over back.

Temperament: As the sole purpose of the Shih Tzu is that of a companion and house pet, it is essential that its temperament be outgoing, happy, affectionate, friendly and trusting towards all.

Approved May 9, 1989
Effective June 29, 1989

Meet the Silky Terrier

Recognized by AKC® in 1959
Silky Terrier Club of America (silkyterrierclubofamerica.org), formed in 1955

Traits
- Bold
- Energetic
- Quick

HISTORY

Known originally as the "Sydney Silky," this small but sturdy toy breed is the result of the mating of a Yorkshire Terrier and an Australian Terrier in the early twentieth century. Delving farther back into their history, we find a scrappy Tasmanian ratter known as the "Broken-coated Terrier" as the forerunner of both native Australian terrier breeds. Furthermore, DNA tests indicate the presence of several other breeds, including the Cairn and Dandie Dinmont Terriers. In 1903, the Kennel Club of New South Wales wrote the first standard for the Silky-haired Terrier.

The breed made its way to America in the 1950s, and within four years, a Silky puppy turned up on the cover of a newspaper supplement called This Week. A California dog fancier, Evelyn Holaday saw the picture and was smitten. And so, Sir Boomerang, a six-week-old Silky puppy, boarded a Qantas flight in Sydney and traveled 7,500 miles to a new world. A year later, the Sydney Silky Terrier Club of America was formed, and the little dogs became popular as magazine models. In early US shows, they were often mistaken for oversize Yorkies, but over the following decades, breeders successfully established a Silky type, distinct from either of the foundation breeds.

FORM AND FUNCTION

These companion dogs are sturdy and rectangular in shape, and their crowning glory is their straight, single glossy coat, which feels a lot like human hair. As breeder Linda Gross wrote in The Silky Terrier Times, recalling her first glimpse of one, "The dog's hair was spectacular: liquid silver tipped in black, rich browns and golden tans." The hair is to be parted in the middle, so that it cascades down on each side, presenting a "well groomed by not sculptured appearance." Unlike the Yorkie, however, it should not reach the ground. The desired "piercingly keen" appearance is further enhanced by the dog's small, erect, V-shaped ears.

LIVING WITH A SILKY

Other than their hair, Silkies behave and look more like their ancestors from the terrier side of the family. Intelligent, bold, and energetic, they need human partners who will know how to channel that energy into daily exercise and training for sports and work. At least one Silky earned his keep as a mold-detection dog. Breeders warn that Silkies are so cute that people may be tempted to let them get away with undesirable behaviors. Owners must be strong and make sure they set rules and stick to them. Like most breeds with terrier in their genes, Silkies can't resist a good varmint chase, and they are speedy. Leashes are essential when walking outside. Grooming is fairly easy, requiring regular bathing and brushing.

COMPETITION

Silkies do well in the conformation ring and have been successful in companion events, particularly agility. They were the first toy breed to be approved to compete in earthdog events.

Official Standard for the Silky Terrier

General Appearance: The Silky Terrier is a true "toy terrier." He is moderately low set, slightly longer than tall, of refined bone structure, but of sufficient substance to suggest the ability to hunt and kill domestic rodents. His coat is silky in texture, parted from the stop to the tail and presents a well groomed but not sculptured appearance. His inquisitive nature and joy of life make him an ideal companion.

Size, Proportion, Substance: *Size*—Shoulder height from 9 to 10 inches. Deviation in either direction is undesirable. *Proportion*—The body is about one-fifth longer than the dog's height at the withers. *Substance*—Lightly built with strong but rather fine bone.

Head: The head is strong, wedge-shaped, and moderately long. *Expression* piercingly keen, *eyes* small, dark, almond shaped with dark rims. Light eyes are a serious fault. *Ears* are small, V-shaped, set high and carried erect without any tendency to flare obliquely off the skull. *Skull* flat, and not too wide between the ears. The skull is slightly longer than the muzzle. *Stop* shallow. The *nose* is black. *Teeth* strong and well aligned, scissors bite. An undershot or overshot bite is a serious fault.

Neck, Topline and Body: The *neck* fits gracefully into sloping shoulders. It is medium long, fine, and to some degree crested. The *topline* is level. A topline

Silky Terrier

showing a roach or dip is a serious fault. **Chest** medium wide and deep enough to extend down to the elbows. The *body* is moderately low set and about one-fifth longer than the dog's height at the withers. The body is measured from the point of the shoulder (or forechest) to the rearmost projection of the upper thigh (or point of the buttocks). A body which is too short is a fault, as is a body which is too long. The tail is docked, set high and carried at twelve to two o'clock position.

Forequarters: Well laid back shoulders, together with proper angulation at the upper arm, set the forelegs nicely under the body. Forelegs are strong, straight and rather fine-boned. *Feet* small, catlike, round, compact. Pads are thick and springy while nails are strong and dark colored. White or flesh-colored nails are a fault. The feet point straight ahead, with no turning in or out. Dewclaws, if any, are removed.

Hindquarters: Thighs well muscled and strong, but not so developed as to appear heavy. Well angulated stifles with low hocks which are parallel when viewed from behind. *Feet* as in front.

Coat: Straight, single, glossy, silky in texture. On matured specimens the coat falls below and follows the body outline. It should not approach floor length. On the top of the head, the hair is so profuse as to form a topknot, but long hair on the face and ears is objectionable. The hair is parted on the head and down over the back to the root of the tail. The tail is well coated but devoid of plume. Legs should have short hair from the pastern and hock joints to the feet. The feet should not be obscured by the leg furnishings.

Color: Blue and tan. The blue may be silver blue, pigeon blue or slate blue, the tan deep and rich. The blue extends from the base of the skull to the tip of the tail, down the forelegs to the elbows, and halfway down the outside of the thighs. On the tail the blue should be very dark. Tan appears on muzzle and cheeks, around the base of the ears, on the legs and feet and around the vent. The topknot should be silver or fawn which is lighter than the tan points.

Gait: Should be free, light-footed, lively and straightforward. Hindquarters should have strong propelling power. Toeing in or out is to be faulted.

Temperament: The keenly alert air of the terrier is characteristic, with shyness or excessive nervousness to be faulted. The manner is quick, friendly, responsive.

Approved October 10, 1989
Effective November 30, 1989

Meet the Toy Fox Terrier

Recognized by AKC® in 2003
American Toy Fox Terrier Club (atftc.com), formed in 1994

Traits
- Playful
- Friendly
- Eager to Please

HISTORY

This bright little companion dog was truly "made in the U. S. A.," created by mixing Smooth Fox Terriers with well-established toy breeds, including Miniature Pinschers, Italian Greyhounds, Chihuahuas, and Toy Manchester Terriers. A runt in a litter of Smooth Fox Terriers, born in the 1930s, is said to have been the inspiration behind the development of this terrier in a tiny package. The breed combines the feistiness of its larger hunting cousins with the companionable nature and sweetness of a toy dog, nicknamed the Ameritoy, shorthand for "American Toy." Small size and intelligence combined with the tendency to be a show-off made these dogs perfect performers alongside circus clowns—small, agile, and smart enough to learn how to walk a tightrope.

FORM AND FUNCTION

Graceful, muscular, and elegant are just a few of the words used to describe the physique of these lap-sized charmers. Only 8.5 to 11.5 inches at the shoulder, fanciers say these dogs are both a "toy and a terrier," possessing some of the best qualities of both. Despite having a toy's build, they should give a terrier's impression of effortless movement and endless endurance, as well as strength and stamina, as noted in the breed standard. This allows the dog to fill several roles, from a great hunter of mice and other small vermin to a gentle companion to curl up in the lap of an elderly owner. Other defining traits are the smooth, satiny coat; the upright, pointed, inverted V-shaped ears; and the bright dark eyes, for an expression of alert intelligence.

LIVING WITH A TOY FOX

With their blend of toy and terrier temperament, a Toy Fox Terrier can spend a day dashing around the yard, chasing balls and birds, then happily snuggle on the couch all evening. They are extremely playful through their long lives (about thirteen to fifteen years). They also know how to turn down the volume, but not the charm, for quieter times. They are naturally extroverted and highly intelligent, which makes training, including housetraining, a breeze. Keep in mind, though, that they are very sensitive and will learn best with positive methods. Their short, tight coats make them easy keepers as far as grooming is concerned, needing just a light brushing two or three times a week. The downside of their short hair is that they may need a sweater in winter.

COMPETITION

Toy Fox Terriers are eligible to compete in conformation, companion events, and earthdog events, and they make excellent therapy dogs.

Official Standard for the Toy Fox Terrier

General Appearance: The Toy Fox Terrier is truly a toy and a terrier and both have influenced his personality and character. As a terrier, the Toy Fox Terrier possesses keen intelligence, courage, and animation. As a toy he is diminutive, and devoted with an endless abiding love for his master. The Toy Fox Terrier is a well-balanced toy dog of athletic appearance displaying grace and agility in equal measure with strength and stamina. His lithe muscular body has a smooth elegant outline which conveys the impression of effortless movement and endless endurance. He is naturally well groomed, proud, animated, and alert. Characteristic traits are his elegant head, his short glossy and predominantly white coat, coupled with a predominantly solid head, and his short high-set tail.

Size, Proportion, Substance: *Size*—8½ to 11½ inches, 9 to 11 preferred, 8½ to 11½ acceptable. *Proportion*—The Toy Fox Terrier is square in proportion, with height being approximately equal to length; with height measured from withers to ground and length measured from point of shoulder to buttocks. Slightly longer in bitches is acceptable. *Substance*—Bone must be strong, but not excessive and always in proportion to size. Overall balance is important. Disqualification: Any dog under 8½ inches and over 11½ inches.

Head: The head is elegant, balanced and expressive with no indication of coarseness. *Expression* is intelligent, alert, eager and full of interest. *Eyes:* Clear, bright and dark, including eye-rims, with the exception of chocolates whose eye-rims should be self-colored. The eyes are full, round and somewhat prominent, yet never bulging, with a soft intelligent expression. They are set well apart, not slanted, and fit well together into the sockets. *Ears:* The ears are erect, pointed, inverted V-shaped, set high and close together, but never touching. The size is in proportion to the head and body. Disqualification:

Ears not erect on any dog over six months of age. **Skull:** Is moderate in width, slightly rounded and softly wedge shaped. Medium stop, somewhat sloping. When viewed from the front, the head widens gradually from the nose to the base of the ears. The distance from the nose to the stop is equal to the distance from the stop to the occiput. The cheeks are flat and muscular, with the area below the eyes well filled in. Faults: Apple head. **Muzzle:** Strong rather than fine, in proportion to the head as a whole and parallel to the top of the skull. **Nose:** Black only with the exception of self-colored in chocolate dogs. Disqualification: Dudley nose. **Lips:** Are small and tight fitting. **Bite:** A full complement of strong white teeth meeting in a scissors bite is preferred. Loss of teeth should not be faulted as long as the bite can be determined as correct. Disqualification: Undershot, wry mouth, overshot more than $\frac{1}{8}$ inch.

Neck, Topline, Body: The *neck* is carried proudly erect, well set on, slightly arched, gracefully curved, clean, muscular and free from throatiness. It is proportioned to the head and body and widens gradually blending smoothly into the shoulders. The length of the neck is approximately the same as that of the head. The *topline* is level when standing and gaiting. The *body* is balanced and tapers slightly from ribs to flank. The *chest* is deep and muscular with well sprung ribs. Depth of chest extends to the point of elbow. The *back* is straight, level, and muscular. Short and strong in loin with moderate tuck-up to denote grace and elegance. The *croup* is level with topline and well-rounded. The *tail* is set high, held erect and in proportion to the size of the dog. Docked to the third or fourth joint.

Forequarters: Forequarters are well angulated. The shoulder is firmly set and has adequate muscle, but is not overdeveloped. The shoulders are sloping and well laid back, blending smoothly from neck to back. The forechest is well developed. The elbows are close and perpendicular to the body. The legs are parallel and straight to the pasterns which are strong and straight while remaining flexible. Feet are small and oval, pointing forward turning neither in nor out. Toes are strong, well-arched and closely knit with deep pads.

Hindquarters: Hindquarters are well angulated, strong and muscular. The upper and lower thighs are strong, well muscled and of good length. The stifles are clearly defined and well angulated. Hock joints are well let down and firm. The rear pasterns are straight. The legs are parallel from the rear and turn neither in nor out. Dewclaws should be removed from hindquarters if present.

Coat: The coat is shiny, satiny, fine in texture and smooth to the touch. It is slightly longer in the ruff, uniformly covering the body.

Color: *Tri-Color:* Predominately black head with sharply defined tan markings on cheeks, lips and eye dots. Body is over 50 percent white, with or without black body spots. *White, Chocolate and Tan*: Predominately chocolate head with sharply defined tan markings on cheeks, lips and eye dots. Body is over 50 percent white, with or without chocolate body spots. *White and Tan*: Predominately tan head. Body is over 50 percent white with or without tan body spots. ***White and Black***: Predominately black head. Body is over 50 percent white with or without black body spots. Color should be rich and clear. Blazes are acceptable, but may not touch the eyes or ears. Clear white is preferred, but a small amount of ticking is not to be penalized. Body spots on black-headed tri-colors must be black; body spots on chocolate-headed tri-colors must be chocolate; both with or without a slight fringe of tan alongside any body spots near the chest and under the tail as seen in normal bi-color patterning. Faults: Color, other than ticking, that extends below the elbow or the hock. Disqualifications: A blaze extending into the eyes or ears. Any color combination not stated above. Any dog whose head is more than 50 percent white. Any dog whose body is not more than 50 percent white. Any dog whose head and body spots are of different colors.

Gait: Movement is smooth and flowing with good reach and strong drive. The topline should remain straight and head and tail carriage erect while gaiting. Fault: Hackney gait.

Temperament: The Toy Fox Terrier is intelligent, alert and friendly, and loyal to its owners. He learns new tasks quickly, is eager to please, and adapts to almost any situation. The Toy Fox Terrier, like other terriers, is self-possessed, spirited, determined and not easily intimidated. He is a highly animated toy dog that is comical, entertaining and playful all of his life. Any individuals lacking good terrier attitude and personality are to be faulted.

Disqualifications: Any dog under 8½ inches or over 11½ inches. Ears not erect on any dog over six months of age. Dudley nose. Undershot, wry mouth, overshot more than ⅛ inch. A blaze extending into the eyes or ears. Any color combination not stated above. Any dog whose head is more than 50 percent white. Any dog whose body is not more than 50 percent white. Any dog whose head and body spots are of different colors.

Approved July 8, 2003
Effective August 27, 2003

Meet the Yorkshire Terrier

Recognized by AKC® in 1885
Yorkshire Terrier Club of America (theyorkshireterrierclubofamerica.org), formed in 1951

Traits
- Affectionate
- Spirited
- Bossy

Yorkshire Terrier

AKC Official Guide to Toy Dogs

Yorkshire Terrier

HISTORY

It seems odd that a dog prized around the world as the quintessential lady's pet—all button eyes, silky hair, bows, and oh, so dainty—was created for the decidedly unglamorous job of killing rats, but that is how the Yorkshire Terrier came to be. Although there are no firm records, the ancestors of this charming breed were likely a mix of Scottish and English terriers, brought together when Scottish weavers immigrated into the Yorkshire area of England in the mid-1800s. The weavers needed a dog to keep their factories free of vermin. To work in the looms, a dog had to be small in size and lethal on rats—laborers did not have a lot of money to spend on feeding large animals. Originally, these tiny dogs were known as Broken-haired Scottish Terriers and weighed about 14 pounds. Around 1870, they became known as Yorkshire Terriers, and breeders stabilized the signature coat—a silky blue and tan cascade of shiny hair, parted in the middle of the back.

By the late nineteenth century, Yorkies had made it to America and were exhibited at the Westminster Kennel Club dog show, but they weren't winning any popularity contests and settled into the middle of the AKC® registration lists. Then, in 1944, Smoky came along. She was a tiny Yorkie, only about 7 inches tall, that somehow had been left in the jungles of New Guinea. American G.I. William A. Wynne adopted the little dog, and she accompanied him, in his backpack, all through the Pacific Theater, more than once saving his life. After the war, Wynne wrote a book—Yorkie Doodle Dandy—about his little "angel from a foxhole." This unlikely war dog, and the adorable photos of her sleeping in Wynne's helmet, won American hearts. More interest came with a celebrity fancier, movie star Audrey Hepburn, and by 1960, Yorkies were on the way to becoming one of America's most popular dogs. Today, these bright little terriers are routinely in the top ten in popularity, and in some cities, such as New York, have nudged the Labrador Retriever out of first place.

FORM AND FUNCTION

Compact and sturdy, the coat is the breed's signature trait. It must be long and shiny, giving the appearance of a piece of silk, and of distinctive colors, a metallic steel blue cascading from a part that starts at the back of the head and extends to the root of the tail, with a rich golden tan on the head, legs, chest, and breeches. Puppies who develop the correct coloring for the show ring are always born black with tan markings.

LIVING WITH A YORKIE

Although diminutive and delicate, Yorkies are spirited dogs, true to their working-terrier roots. They do not seem to realize how small they are. Without strong leadership, they have a tendency to become bossy, especially if their owners allow them to get away with naughty behaviors—like yapping and pulling—that would never be acceptable in a larger dog. It is imperative that the Yorkie owner gives the dog boundaries and solid training, and a moderate amount of exercise. They are great apartment dogs and a favorite among city dwellers because their size makes exercise a snap: a game of catch in the living room could easily tire a Yorkie out. A Yorkie's coat requires a good deal of daily attention to avoid mats and maintain the shine. As with all small dogs, it's important to pay attention to dental hygiene. Generally easy to care for, Yorkies have a long life span, on average twelve to fifteen years.

COMPETITION

Yorkshire Terriers are superb conformation dogs and also compete in companion events, including obedience, agility, and the coursing ability test. With proper socialization and training, they make exquisite therapy dogs.

Official Standard for the Yorkshire Terrier

General Appearance: That of a long-haired toy terrier whose blue and tan coat is parted on the face and from the base of the skull to the end of the tail and hangs evenly and quite straight down each side of body. The body is neat, compact and well proportioned. The dog's high head carriage and confident manner should give the appearance of vigor and self-importance.

Head: Small and rather flat on top, the *skull* not too prominent or round, the *muzzle* not too long, with the *bite* neither undershot nor overshot and teeth sound. Either scissors bite or level bite is acceptable. The *nose* is black. *Eyes* are medium in size and not too prominent; dark in color and sparkling with a sharp, intelligent expression. Eye rims are dark. Ears are small, V-shaped, carried erect and set not too far apart.

Body: Well proportioned and very compact. The back is rather short, the back line level, with height at shoulder the same as at the rump.

Legs and Feet: *Forelegs* should be straight, elbows neither in nor out. *Hind legs* straight when viewed from behind, but stifles are moderately bent when viewed from the sides. *Feet* are round with black toenails. Dewclaws, if any, are generally removed from the hind legs. Dewclaws on the forelegs may be removed.

Tail: Docked to a medium length and carried slightly higher than the level of the back.

Coat: Quality, texture and quantity of coat are of prime importance. Hair is glossy, fine and silky in texture. Coat on the body is moderately long and perfectly straight (not wavy). It may be trimmed to floor length to give ease of movement and a neater appearance, if desired. The fall on the head is long, tied with one bow in center of head or parted in the middle and tied with two bows. Hair on muzzle is very long. Hair should be trimmed short on tips of ears and may be trimmed on feet to give them a neat appearance.

Colors: Puppies are born black and tan and are normally darker in body color, showing an intermingling of black hair in the tan until they

Yorkshire Terrier

are matured. Color of hair on body and richness of tan on head and legs are of prime importance in adult dogs, to which the following color requirements apply:

Blue—Is a dark steel-blue, not a silver-blue and not mingled with fawn, bronzy or black hairs.

Tan—All tan hair is darker at the roots than in the middle, shading to still lighter tan at the tips. There should be no sooty or black hair intermingled with any of the tan.

Color on body—The blue extends over the body from back of neck to root of tail. Hair on tail is a darker blue, especially at end of tail.

Head fall—A rich golden tan, deeper in color at sides of head, at ear roots and on the muzzle, with ears a deep rich tan. Tan color should not extend down on back of neck.

Chest and legs—A bright, rich tan, not extending above the elbow on the forelegs nor above the stifle on the hind legs.

Weight: Must not exceed 7 pounds.

Disqualifications: Any solid color or combination of colors other than blue and tan as described above. Any white markings other than a small white spot on the forechest that does not exceed 1 inch at its longest dimension.

Approved July 10, 2007
Effective October 1, 2007

Index

A

Affenpinscher, **36–39**
agility tests, 30–31
AKC® Canine Health Foundation (CHF), 12
AKC® Canine Partners, 14
AKC® Education, 13
AKC® Family Dog (magazine), 13
The AKC® Gazette (magazine), 13
AKC® Humane Fund Award for Canine Excellence (ACE), 14
AKC® Humane Fund, 12, 14, 25
AKC® Inspections, 12
AKC Meet the Breeds®, 13
AKC® Museum of the Dog, 13
AKC Rally®, 32
AKC® Reunite, 12
AKC Scent Work®, 32
AKC.org, 13
American Kennel Club® (AKC®)
   about: origins and overview, 10
   building community, 13–14
   founding and mission of, 10
   health and welfare advancement, 12
   organizations of, 12–14
   recognizing greatness, 14
   registering puppy, 25
anatomy of a dog, 16–20
   about: overview of, 16
   by breed (*See specific breeds*)
   breed standards by body part, 18–20

B

Biewer Terrier, 22, **40–44**
bite, general standards, 18. *See also specific breeds*
body parts, breed standards (general), 18–20. *See also specific breeds*
Breeder of the Year Award (AKC®), 14
breeders, choosing/considerations, 24–25, 26, 27. *See also* puppy(ies)
Brussels Griffon, 6, **45–49**

C

Canine Good Citizen®/S.T.A.R. Puppy®, 32
Cavalier King Charles Spaniel, 5, 24, **50–54**
Chihuahua, 9, 10–11, **55–59**
Chinese Crested, **60–63**

coat, standards. *See specific breeds*
color, standards. *See specific breeds*
community, AKC® building, 13–14
competition. *See specific breeds*; standards by body part
conformation events, 29

D

disqualification criteria. *See specific breeds*

E

ears, general standards, 18. *See also specific breeds*
education, AKC®, 13
English Toy Spaniel, **64–67**
excellence award, AKC® Humane Fund Award for Canine Excellence (ACE), 14

F

Fast CAT®, 32, 33
feet, general standards, 18
forequarters, standards. *See specific breeds*
form and function of breeds. *See specific breeds*
front assembly, general standards, 18. *See also specific breeds*

G

gait, standards. *See specific breeds*
good citizen. *See* Canine Good Citizen®
greyhound. *See* Italian Greyhound

H

Havanese, 9, 13, **68–72**
head, general standards, 18. *See also specific breeds*
health and welfare, AKC® services, 12
hindquarters, standards. *See specific breeds*
history
   AKC® origins, 5
   sports and activities overview, 28
   of toy breeds, 5 (*See also specific breeds*)
Humane Fund Award for Canine Excellence, AKC®, 14

I

inspections, AKC®, 12
Italian Greyhound, **73–76**

J

Japanese Chin, **77–81**
Junior Showmanship program, 29

L

Lifetime Achievement Awards, AKC®, 14
living with various breeds. *See* puppy(ies); *specific breeds*
lost pets, reuniting with owners, 12

M

magazines, award-winning, 13
Maltese, 12, 34–35, **82–85**
Manchester Terrier (Toy), **86–90**
Miniature Pinscher, 16–17, **91–95**
museum, AKC® Museum of the Dog, 13

O

obedience exercises, 30

P

Papillon, 20, 32, **96–100**
parent clubs, 25
Pekingese, **101–5**
pinschers. *See* Affenpinscher; Miniature Pinscher
Pomeranian, 23, 30–31, **106–10**
Poodle (Toy), 25, 33, **111–15**
proportion, size, substance standards. *See specific breeds*
public events, AKC®, 13
Pug, 19, 27, **116–19**
puppy(ies), 21–26
    breed selection, 22
    breeder considerations, 24–25, 26, 27
    considerations for getting, 22
    contacting parent clubs before getting, 25
    registering, 25
    S.T.A.R. Puppy®, 32

R

rally, AKC Rally®, 32
rear assembly, general standards, 20. *See also specific breeds*
registering puppy, 25
reuniting pets with owners, 12
rib cage, general standards, 20. *See also specific breeds*
Russian Toy, 15, **120–24**

S

Scent Work®, AKC, 32
Search and Rescue (SAR), 32
Shih Tzu, 21, **125–28**
Silky Terrier, 9, **129–33**
size, proportion, substance standards. *See specific breeds*
spaniels. *See* Cavalier King Charles Spaniel; English Toy Spaniel
sports and activities
    about: history and overview of, 28
    age range of human participants, 29
    agility tests, 30–31
    AKC Rally®, 32
    Canine Good Citizen®/S.T.A.R. Puppy®, 32
    conformation events, 29
    Fast CAT®, 32, 33
    Junior Showmanship program, 29
    obedience exercises, 30
    range of, 28
    Search and Rescue (SAR), 32
    standards by body part and, 18–20 (*See also specific breeds*)
    tracking and AKC Scent Work®, 30–32
standards by body part, 18–20. *See also specific breeds*
S.T.A.R. Puppy®, 32
substance, size, proportions standards. *See specific breeds*

T

tails, general standards, 20. *See also specific breeds*
temperament, standards. *See specific breeds*
terriers. *See* Biewer Terrier; Manchester Terrier (Toy); Silky Terrier; Toy Fox Terrier; Yorkshire Terrier
toy breeds
    about: historical perspective, 5; overview of, 34
    Affenpinscher, **36–39**
    Biewer Terrier, 22, **40–44**
    Brussels Griffon, 6, **45–49**
    Cavalier King Charles Spaniel, 5, 24, **50–54**
    Chihuahua, 9, 10–11, **55–59**
    Chinese Crested, **60–63**
    English Toy Spaniel, **64–67**
    Havanese, 9, 13, **68–72**
    Italian Greyhound, **73–76**
    Japanese Chin, **77–81**
    Maltese, 12, 34–35, **82–85**
    Manchester Terrier (Toy), **86–90**
    Miniature Pinscher, 16–17, **91–95**
    Papillon, 20, 32, **96–100**
    Pekingese, **101–5**
    Pomeranian, 23, 30–31, **106–10**
    Poodle (Toy), 25, 33, **111–15**
    Pug, 19, 27, **116–19**
    Russian Toy, 15, **120–24**
    Shih Tzu, 21, **125–28**
    Silky Terrier, 9, **129–33**
    Toy Fox Terrier, **134–38**
    Yorkshire Terrier, 2–3, **139–42**
Toy Fox Terrier, **134–38**
tracking and AKC Scent Work®, 30–32
traits by breed. *See specific breeds*

W

website, AKC.org, 13

Y

Yorkshire Terrier, 2–3, **139–42**